D0880832

Pulse

Richard,
   I hope you like
these buzz-metrics!

[signature]

Pulse

The New Science of Harnessing Internet Buzz to Track Threats and Opportunities

DOUGLAS W. HUBBARD

WILEY

John Wiley & Sons, Inc.

Published by John Wiley & Sons, Inc., Hoboken, New Jersey.
Published simultaneously in Canada.

For general information on our other products and services or for technical support,
please contact our Customer Care Department within the United States at
(800) 762-2974, outside the United States at (317) 572-3993 or fax (317) 572-4002.

Wiley also publishes its books in a variety of electronic formats. Some content that
appears in print may not be available in electronic books. For more information about
Wiley products, visit our web site at www.wiley.com.

Library of Congress Cataloging-in-Publication Data:

Hubbard, Douglas W., 1962–
    Pulse: the new science of harnessing internet buzz to track threats and
opportunities / Douglas W. Hubbard.
        p. cm.
    Includes index.
      ISBN 978-0-470-93236-0 (cloth); ISBN 978-111-8-06376-7 (ebk);
      ISBN 978-111-8-06377-4 (ebk); ISBN 978-111-8-06378-1 (ebk)
    1. Marketing research–Computer network resources.   2. Internet research.
  3. Business forecasting.   I. Title.
      HF5415.2.H7775 2011
      658.8′302854678–dc22

                                                                    2010050399

Printed in the United States of America

10 9 8 7 6 5 4 3 2 1

My dedication for my third book is very similar to my earlier books. I am entirely motivated to write for and by my family: Janet, Evan, Madeleine, and Steven.

And once again, I would also like to dedicate this to my personal friends and colleagues in all branches of the U.S. Military for all their sacrifices.

Contents

Preface

I first started thinking about a book on this topic when I finished writing the first edition of my first book—*How to Measure Anything: Finding the Value of Intangibles in Business* (John Wiley & Sons)—in late 2006. One chapter was titled "New Measurement Instruments for Management," where I talked about the possibility of farming data from the Internet for practical business measurements. I wondered about such possibilities as using data about home sales published on sites like realtor.com or eBay to inform us—on a real-time basis—about that part of the economy.

Sometime in 2007 I learned about the tool Google Trends—a tool which shows how frequently certain search terms are used in Google. After the darkest days of the financial crisis in 2008, I became more interested in seeing if financial trends like this could have shown up in our search behavior on the Internet. At one point I typed "unemployment" into the Google Trends tool and compared it to the official unemployment figures from the Bureau of Labor Statistics. The patterns matched very closely, but what was really amazing was that the Google Trends data was available a month before the official data came out. I was hooked and started searching for more interesting ways that this free data source from Google could track useful economic trends—only much faster than the official economic reports.

Early in 2009, I started finding published research that had already been done on how Internet search data could be applied to forecasting economic trends and flu outbreaks. It seemed as if the frequency of articles like this published in respected, peer-reviewed economic journals was speeding up, and then I noticed that the popular science magazines *New Scientist* and *Science News* were beginning to report this sort of research about once a month or so. It looked like a critical mass was approaching.

Just within the last 24 months leading up to the publication of this book, the research really seemed to be accelerating, and more conferences were being held on the topic of using the Internet as a research tool. Finally, I told my publisher that I felt I had to write this book before someone else did. No one source discussed the recent research in all the different areas using data available on the Internet about our searches, relationships, and daily activities.

As you would expect, different researchers specialized in different aspects of this emerging field. I also found that many researchers were not even aware of work based on different methods of using the Internet. People who were experts at analyzing the text on Twitter to predict macro-trends were generally not aware of the research using location-based services on cell phones, while those experts, in turn, were not aware of research using tools like Google Trends or Yahoo!.

This new field could be served, I thought, by identifying its multiple different components and how they are each used to track big trends. I divided up the kinds of tools along the lines of how we spend our time on the Internet: We search for information, we connect with others, we post our thoughts, we track and share our location, we buy things, and we play games. These are somewhat overlapping since some involve similar technologies, and they sometimes forecast or track similar things.

One of my biggest challenges in writing this book was the same as my other books: What do we call this new thing? One existing name for this field of research—computational social science—sometimes seems to be more specifically associated with social networks, which is only part of what I'm writing about in this book. I think that label is evolving and may eventually be the generally accepted term for all the areas of research I am writing about. In the meantime, I like the metaphor of a pulse. It is as if the combined system of the Internet and the people using it are a kind of organism. It has a rhythm, and if we can track that rhythm, we will see what was previously invisible to psychologists, economists, epidemiologists, law enforcement, linguists, anthropologists, and businesses. This mass of data from what is now about 2 billion Internet users will revolutionize these fields. This new measurement instrument will have as profound an impact for the social sciences as did the microscope for biology, the telescope for astronomy, or the radar and the satellite for meteorology.

Acknowledgments

I would like to thank the following people for helping make this a better book. Some are researchers who have taken the time to speak with me about their important research. Others are colleagues inside and out of this field who have given valuable input to this work on issues related to technology. Some are my analysts who have helped compile a lot of data. Thanks.

Gunther Eysenbach, University of Toronto
Bryan Routledge, Carnegie Mellon University
Brendan O'Connor, Carnegie Mellon University
Ramnath Balasubramanyan, Carnegie Mellon University
Noah Smith, Carnegie Mellon University
Mark Barros, Metric Junkie
Christina Carbone, European Commission Joint Research Center
Marshal Van Alstyne, Boston University
Nathan Eagle, txteagle Inc. and MIT Media Lab
Johan Bollen, Indiana University–Bloomington
Bing Pan, College of Charleston
Gregor Orelind, Alexa
Angela Lipscomb, SAS
Jeff Gilleland, SAS
John Bastone, SAS
Michael Bergines, eBay
Neel Sundaresan, eBay
Alan Mislove, Northeastern University

And my research assistants:
Michael North, Ashley Hubbard, and Joseph Hubbard

PART I

Introduction to the Pulse: A New Kind of Instrument

CHAPTER 1

A New Era for Measuring and Predicting Society

The digital traces of you and everyone you know are transforming our understanding of human behavior.
> —*New Scientist*, July 24, 2010

Something important is changing in how we as a society use computers to mine data. . . . As more diverse sensors become pervasive, wireless networking becomes more widespread, and new algorithms are developed, a global sensor network monitoring much of humanity might emerge.
> —Tom Mitchel of Carnegie Mellon as quoted in, S*cience,* December 2009

The first half of the twenty-first century is seeing the emergence of a new type of scientific instrument that will measure the biggest and most important trends in society. More people spend more time doing more things online and as they do so, they leave behind a vast digital record. By using the combined "digital footprints" of the entire world, sociologists, psychologists, economists, and even physicians are learning to measure aspects of our society that would otherwise be virtually invisible. The analysis of these digital traces will generate new discoveries in every area of research that uses it. The volume of the data will detect new patterns in markets, public opinions, and even health and safety—and the information will be available fast enough to be actionable.

Publicly available data about the frequency of certain searches on Google have been used to track flu outbreaks, consumer confidence, or unemployment levels faster than the government authorities are able to do so. The analysis of millions of "Tweets" on the micro-blogging site Twitter have been used to predict the popularity of a movie, presidential approval ratings and even stock market moves. Classified ads on sites like Craigslist correlate with home foreclosures and unemployment. Data gathered passively from mobile phones can be used to track traffic patterns, illness, and even damage after an earthquake. And this is just the beginning.

Even reserved scientists describe this phenomenon as a revolution in the study of humanity and in the forecasting of humanity's large-scale behavior. These tools will fundamentally change how we track threats and opportunities. Ultimately, this new source of data will influence how some of the most important decisions are made by individuals, businesses and governments.

Only relatively recently have researchers been discovering how to track economic trends, flu outbreaks, and public opinions by using publicly available data left behind by a couple of billion Internet and mobile phone users. These digital footprints are left by the people of the world as they use the Internet and mobile phones to blog, buy things, search for information, connect with other people, and even as they play online. This vast data set is the first opportunity for many of the social sciences to work with a quantity of detailed statistics that rivals or even exceeds the data sets of, say, particle physics or astronomy. Just as weather forecasting becomes more accurate with increased numbers of sensors and improved computational power, forecasting the "weather" of society will become just as scientific.

The weather map analogy works at many levels. The real value of weather maps is not in seeing where the weather patterns are right now; it is in seeing where the weather *will be*. And the more macroscopic the map, the better able we will be to see the trends. Likewise, many of the threats that we have faced in the first decades after 2000—terrorism, financial chaos, epidemics, and more—could be better seen in advance if we had a kind of macro-level weather map for society. And many opportunities will be apparent only if we can see where the big trends are leading business or public opinion.

Individual observations about where someone lives or the output of one small business say almost nothing about big trends. You can't see the size and shape of a storm by examining a few raindrops; similarly, you can't see big changes in the economy or society by looking only at your own neighbors or coworkers. However, a vast number of these data points can show us patterns on a large scale.

The Internet has been used for great business opportunities, as a repository of all human knowledge, as the means of collaboration across the globe, and as the ultimate tool of public dialogue. *However, a few initial examples from academia notwithstanding—the Internet itself is almost entirely underutilized as a measurement instrument of society.* The primary method of tracking big trends in society is still the survey and, in the case of business, the system of financial reports. Business and governments understand the significance of using these traditional surveys to inform critical strategies.

By 2002, the U.S. Government alone was spending over $4 billion per year on surveys to measure the economy and other aspects of society. The commercial sector was spending about $15 billion per year on the same.[1]

Traditional survey methods involve carefully designed studies that allow for straightforward statistical analysis. Unfortunately, they are expensive, slow, and—even with the rigorous methodologies—often don't capture what is really happening. They are plagued with small response rates, and in some cases what people say on surveys has little to do with reality. These methods often take weeks to months for the report to be finished—many times this is long after the data would have been useful. A striking example of the lack of timeliness of existing analytical methods was when the National Bureau of Economic Research (NBER) reported in September 2010 that the Great Recession had ended 15 months prior. Surely there is room for improvement.

The Internet is already many orders of magnitude larger than all the data collected by governments and businesses using traditional surveys. The social networking site Facebook alone processes 25 terabytes of data each day. This is about 1,000 times the amount of data delivered by the U.S. mail daily. The largest survey in the world—the US Census—produces less data than this *in a decade*. In 2010, the microblogging service Twitter gave the Library of Congress 167 terabytes of data representing over 6 billion "tweets." (A tweet is a single string of text, 140 characters or less, posted by one of the over 30 million Twitter users. Each one is a tiny daily diary entry saying something about what that person is thinking and doing.) And these sources still only comprise part of the publically-visible digital data we leave behind.

The data of the Internet is, of course, unstructured and in some ways more difficult to analyze than a purpose-built survey. Fortunately, new methods for analyzing this data scientifically are evolving even as the volume of data continues to grow at a fantastic rate. The collective digital record of our behavior has now grown to a point where it can reflect something useful about the system's users. Now we can see the equivalent of the weather map for public opinion, the economy, our health, and our anxieties.

This Book's Web Presence

This book, in keeping with the spirit of connecting to the Pulse, also has an online presence at www.pulsethenewscience.com. Throughout the book, I defer to the Web site for more elaborate examples of analysis of the Pulse. There, the reader can download spreadsheets and see other examples of the Pulse, including links to recent examples.

An Emerging Science: What Is This New Thing?

This new availability of terabytes of social data and the emerging social science dedicated to analyzing it is too new to even have a widely accepted name. I've considered terms like "social data analytics" or "cybersociology" as names for this science. I've thought about using "digital buzz" or "net pulse" to describe the trends that are made visible with the analysis. Still, these don't seem to fully capture the phenomenon and its magnitude.

Perhaps science fiction got close to the idea. In his 1951 science fiction classic, *Foundation* (Gnome Press Publishers), Isaac Asimov imagined "psychohistory"—a futuristic branch of mathematics applied to history and sociology. He described how it could be used to compute probabilities of macroscopic behaviors in society similar to how a physicist can predict the overall behavior of a gas without predicting the behavior of individual atoms. Pyschohistory seems related to the emerging science this book discusses, but Asimov was vague on the source of data used to feed the formulas of psychohistory. What makes a real science possible is not just the math, but some way to collect the data, preferably a lot of it.

One intriguing term I've heard to refer specifically to the recent availability of the data is "social data revolution" (SDR). This phrase was coined by Andreas Weigend at Stanford University and it seems to encompass the essence of both the new science and the new social phenomenon. His term conveys both the suddenness and magnitude of the availability of social data from sources like Amazon book reviews, Twitter, eBay auctions and Facebook.

His credentials in business, science, and academics give Weigend a unique perspective on this topic. His PhD is in physics and his early work as an undergraduate was at CERN where he analyzed the data coming from particle detectors. This background in the unique challenges of analyzing large amounts of data are what led him to his position as the Chief Scientist of Amazon and later to his position as director of the Social Data Lab at Stanford.

He told me that SDR was first proposed not as a name for some grand new era but simply as the name for a course he was teaching at Stanford. He believed the previous name of the course, "Data Mining and E-Commerce" was too narrow and bland to cover the content the course was evolving into. He explained that his proposed name was accepted as both more comprehensive and inspiring: "In 2009, the department decided 'Social Data Revolution' captures its essence better and renamed the class. It was interesting how the new title attracted more creative, entrepreneurial students."

Another term I like, as you can tell from the title of the book, is simply the capitalized *Pulse*, since this is like the heartbeat of the macro-level

One Small Example of the Pulse

For a quick, concrete example of how to view one tiny aspect of the Pulse online, try this:

1. Go to www.google.com/trends to find the Google Trends site.
2. In the search field, type in the word "coupons."
3. You will see a chart that shows how frequently this term was searched on Google ever since 2004.
4. Note that a sudden increase in searches on this word occurred in the Christmas season in 2007 followed by a bigger spike a year later—at the beginning of the financial crisis in 2008.

This is a simple and useful example of the Pulse because the frequency of searches on this term seems to correlate with certain economic conditions. (People use more coupons when their finances are squeezed.) In Chapter 5, we spend more time on how to interpret and use this data as well as account for other possible explanations for the sudden increase in search activity on this term. Later chapters investigate many other ways to use the Pulse.

behavior of the world. I credit Alan Mislove of Northeastern University in Boston with the first use of the world Pulse in this context (more on him in Chapter 7). Unlike "digital pulse" or "Internet buzz," the term *Pulse* deemphasizes the specific technology and connotes only a single, massive rhythm. However, I may use these terms or perhaps "macro-pulse" to mean about the same things as Weigend's SDR and Mislove's Pulse. I'll define the Pulse and its various synonyms as: *the collective, macroscopic trends which can be scientifically inferred by harnessing publicly accessible data from the Internet.*

Here are three important characteristics of this concept that are both explicit and implied from this definition:

1. *Practical.* In addition to being a powerful tool for academic research, this emerging science has practical applications. The Pulse is computed using sound mathematical methods, but it uses real-world data to solve real-world problems.
2. *Public.* The Internet is the data source. The Pulse is based on all data we leave on the Internet in some form that is publicly accessible, including

data that was initially gathered directly or indirectly by user input or passively gathered by other sensors employed by end users (e.g., the Global Positioning System [GPS] on mobile phones).

3. *Big.* We are focusing on aggregation of the data to spot big, macroscopic patterns and trends, not the identification of individuals or their private data.

If tapping into and using the Pulse seems a little abstract, you can take a quick look at one small example of this Pulse right now. (See "One Small Example of the Pulse.") There are many more ways to access the Pulse than what is shown in this example. Besides analyzing searches on Google, we can analyze auctions on eBay, comments on Twitter, and much more. This is just one concrete example to start with.

What The Pulse Isn't

I explicitly define each of the three attributes as part of the Pulse in order to help distinguish this field from concepts that may be confused with it. The first attribute, practicality, helps to separate this field from some purely theoretical areas of social science that attempt to use mathematical models to describe social interactions. Many theories, even very quantitative ones, already exist for describing the large-scale behavior of groups of individuals. Yet, a theory without data is only half of science.

"Mathematical sociology" has been around since the 1960s. In the 1990s, researchers started using massive computational methods to simulate systems of human interaction. These areas of study became known as computational social science (CSS) or computational sociology. CSS might be part of the academic lineage of the Pulse, but it is not the whole story. Until very recently, CSS had so little data and so much theory it was more of a branch of mathematics than an empirical science. Even key researchers in CSS recognize this fact. (More on this later.)

The requirement of practicality means that the Pulse must support real-world decisions with real-world data. What makes the Pulse an empirical science as opposed to purely a mathematical curiosity is the new availability of data from the Internet. What makes it part of an applied science is how we focus on practical implications for businesses and governments.

Keeping practicality, public availability, and macroscopic scale squarely in mind, we also contrast the Pulse with a few other seemingly related but entirely different concepts. The areas that might be the easiest to confuse with this topic are issues related to the four areas listed next. The other related-sounding topics have already been addressed in plenty of other published material, none of which actually addresses harnessing the Pulse.

What the Pulse Is *Not* (Necessarily or Entirely) Related To
1. Diminishing privacy
2. Using the Internet for lead generation
3. The use of business tools commonly referred to as business intelligence and predictive analytics
4. Online versions of traditional survey methods

The topic of diminishing privacy is one that I frequently find to be associated with the topic of this book. As I speak on this subject at conferences around the United States, I encounter professionals who think that what we are really talking about is the growing intrusion on privacy by tracking our digital footprints. The concern is that exploiting the Pulse necessarily means diminishing privacy and, therefore, we shouldn't use the Pulse for *ethical* reasons. There are two reasons why this particular concern is not justified.

First, almost all of the data needed for this kind of analysis is highly aggregated; individual behaviors are lost. The Google Trends example from "One Small Example of the Pulse" shows nothing of the behavior of individuals. Google may know who is searching for what, but as long as it keeps that information confidential, the rest of us will not be able to see specific searches by other individuals. Whether you or I ever searched on a given term is lost in the data. Yet this highly aggregated data is all we need since we are focusing on the "macro," not the "micro"—the storm front, not the raindrops.

The second issue regarding the privacy concern is that where the data is detailed to the level of particular individuals—such as, for example, a review you write about a book on Amazon using your real name—it is explicitly voluntary. The expectation of privacy does not exist when we choose to use our real names on Twitter, Facebook, Amazon reviews, blogs, and so forth (especially when we include photos and home addresses). The fact is that more and more people are volunteering more information about themselves for public consumption than ever before. You may not be willing to divulge so much private information, but that doesn't mean we shouldn't learn what we can from those who are willing. Visualizing big trends with the Pulse is a way to make good use out of what would otherwise be little more than a cycle of exhibitionism and voyeurism.

At least some of the public is even willing to share their locations through "location-sharing" apps on mobile phones. Again, you may find this is too revealing for your taste, but many thousands—perhaps millions—will volunteer this information, and it can be used for a greater good. Individuals may prefer to reveal their location data for personal convenience (e.g., to have your phone tell you about nearby restaurants you might like or about sales at retail stores). Even so, this data can be shared in a way that doesn't actually reveal individual locations. Like the raindrops in a storm, even this data can be blended together to make the radar map of the storm front. Both laws and technology will change over time in a way that may modify how we can collect data, but aggregation and deliberate volunteering of data will ensure that there is plenty of data to analyze regardless of privacy trends.

Privacy is a different issue from the Pulse, but it is still an important issue—and not just because of threats like identity theft. There are legitimate concerns that the use of vast quantities of social data could be exploited by oppressive regimes. If you are a dictator fearful of a popular resistance, you certainly want access to the Pulse. Evgeny Morozov, author of *The Net Delusion: The Dark Side of Internet Freedom,* argues that anyone who believes that the Internet is only a tool of democracy to feared by authoritarian rulers is a naïve "digital utopian."[2] He uses China and Iran as examples of governments who have effectively used the Internet to track the actions of citizens and to spread propaganda. The mining of social data has already been used against the citizens of a country.

On the other hand, authoritarian regimes sometimes fear social networking technology. Civil revolts in Iran in 2009 and in Tunisia, Egypt, Yemen, and Algeria in 2011 were facilitated by social networks. Egypt's government cut off all Internet and mobile phone service in an attempt to control the organizing power these tools had for protestors. Perhaps with analysis of the Pulse, Egyptian authorities could have *anticipated* the unrest and kept a dictator in power. Like anything else, the Pulse can be used for good or evil. What the reader needs to prepare for is that, either way, the Pulse is happening.

Another area that needs differentiation from the Pulse is various "lead generation" methods and the isolation of individual tweets as news. The Pulse certainty can be used for strategic marketing decisions, but this book doesn't focus on issues like identifying individual leads with data from the Internet. There already is a lot of literature about how to exploit the Internet for lead generation, so there is no need to replicate that body of work.

In a similar vein, many companies already "farm" their online product reviews to try to address proactively negative reactions through direct outreach to disaffected individuals. News organizations also cull blogs and Twitter for public reactions to events and, in some cases, to get wind of new stories. However, in all of these cases, there is a lack of pattern-seeking other than purely anecdotal observations. Again, such an approach focuses on the raindrops instead of the storm front.

Now, if CNN discontinued the segment where it randomly picks tweets that it thinks convey a sentiment about a topic and instead showed a CNN "sentiment index" (SI), then CNN is truly using the Pulse. CNN would report the sentiment index just like it reports the Dow Jones Industrial Average, and it would be validated by being used to predict other measurable phenomenon, such as the results of a traditionally gathered Gallup poll. Journalists could report that the CNN SI on some aspect of the economy is rising slower or faster than expected. Since the SI would be validated by comparison to historical economic trends, it could be an indicator of things to come. Now, that would be much closer to real news.

Exploiting viral marketing methods, however, does seem like a topic worthy of the social data revolution. A "viral" video or Internet myth grows rapidly in a way similar to viruses in the microbiology sense. A person "catches" it from another person, who then passes it on to many others, who each pass it on to many others. Particularly entertaining items, for example, make people want to share them. Viral videos, conspiracy theories, jokes, and news items travel throughout the cyberworld in a way that has patterns—patterns worth investigation for both academic and practical purposes.

Now let's distinguish the Pulse from the analysis of confidential corporate or government databases. The data of interest to us is what could be accessed by the public or could be gathered by anyone—and I'm not talking about security breaches as in the case of Wikileaks in 2010. Confidential data known only to an individual and a company that gathers the information—such as the phone company that has records of your phone calls, or the bank that records financial transactions you specifically make—is very useful to those firms but not to everyone else. It is possible that those firms could use that data to make their own forecasts of the economy or other social trends. Still, since that is not the kind of data most other individuals or firms would have access to, it will be of limited value to decision makers outside of firms that own those databases and it is not considered part of the Pulse.

The public accessibility feature is also a reason why we need to contrast the Pulse with the well-known business tools of data mining, business intelligence (BI), and predictive analytics (PA). Data mining certainly is one of the tools used in the Pulse with the caveat that, in this context, the data mining is entirely outward-looking—searching on the user-generated data available on the Internet—not a review of internal corporate or government files. BI and PA capture part of the spirit of this new science. They are all about analyzing huge amounts of corporate data to try to inform management about the state of the business and possible trends. However, so far, these terms have been used mostly for proprietary and internal databases. Software that has been developed for these purposes eventually will need to combine analysis with the Pulse, and some developers of BI and PA tools have already begun to do so.

Finally, we are not focusing so much on explicit data gathering, such as taking online surveys. There are tools available that are effectively online versions of traditional survey methods. Although the method of administering the survey is, no doubt, much more streamlined than paper-based methods, online surveys are never going to have the same volume of data that Twitter, Google, Facebook, or eBay gather every day. When people are using those sites, they are leaving behind useful information that could be used for BI—but users don't go to those sites just because they want to give some analyst information about their lives.

The Major Areas of the Macro-Pulse

In Part Two, this book examines the world of the digital Pulse by looking at the new tools, methods, and recent research in six broad and overlapping categories of activities. This taxonomy divides the Pulse into areas according to how people leave behind their digital footprints. You can remember the categories in this little rhyme:

Surf, Friend, Say, Go, Buy, and Play.

- *What we surf.* Tools like Google Trends and Google Adwords can be used to determine what the public is searching for. When there is an increase in searches including the words "unemployment" or "coupon," we also see that economic conditions are worsening. How frequently people in one city search on "flu symptoms" has been shown to be a good indicator of where flu outbreaks will occur. There are also tools that tell us about the popularity of specific Web sites. This too tells us something about what people need, want, or fear.
- *Whom we "friend."* "Friend" has become a verb (aka "befriend") in the world of online social networking, and we can use the information you share about who you friend to gather other insights into the structure of society. Using the details of social networks, we can learn about the propagation of gossip and social fads as well as more serious issues like the adoption of new technologies and the spread of diseases. The kinds of social networks people keep tell us something about who they are and what they do. In some cases, the information can even be used to determine criminal threats.
- *What we say.* When we leave our 140-character-long comments on Twitter, comment on a blog, write a customer review for a book, or post a comment on a friend's wall on Facebook, we are leaving behind an important anthropological record of society. What we say in these continuously updated media have been found to agree

closely with Gallup poll research on public opinions of politicians or consumer confidence—but with the added benefit of being nearly real time.

- *Where we go.* A large number of people have already begun to voluntarily transmit their locations from their GPS-equipped mobile phones. Some early research showed that volunteers providing GPS data from mobile phones had entirely different social behaviors from those they had reported on surveys. (This research calls into question many of the findings of traditional survey methods.) Even at a highly aggregated level that reveals nothing about individual locations, this data can be very useful. Where the crowds go may say something about their economic activities and even their opinions and moods.

- *What we buy.* The auctions on a site like eBay are available for anyone to see. By a measure of total items sold, eBay is one of the world's largest retailers, and—unlike most major retailers—it posts every sale it makes the moment the sale is made. The total number of transactions on eBay exceeds the transactions on the New York Stock Exchange and Nasdaq combined. Yet, unlike those financial indexes, eBay presents information about direct consumer purchases. Likewise, Amazon gives us a glimpse of the interests of people when it provides the sales rank of a book (how well that book sells compared to other books). If the Amazon sales ranks of books about, say, buying a new home show that a large number of books on that topic are selling better, this may tell us something about not just what people are doing but what they *intend* to do.

- *How we play.* Perhaps the most underinvestigated area of the macro-Pulse is the collaborative and competitive behavior on sites where we play together. Research shows that our moods do affect the choices we make, even in the games we play. A game session can be considered a rich data stream of individual decisions. Given that some games have millions of players, it is an anthropological record too great to ignore. In addition, there are relatively simple game applications (apps) for Facebook and iPhones. Some of these games have proven to be particularly popular (e.g., Farmville for Facebook). There is even the prospect of creating games *especially* for data collection for the Pulse.

This taxonomy is not perfect, and these areas are not necessarily mutually exclusive or collectively exhaustive. By their nature, many topics of interest could be part of more than one category shown here. Gaming, for example, covers not just what we play but what we buy and say on the Internet. Still, I think this is a good starting point for a very quickly evolving topic. Now in the following paragraphs, we will briefly explore the implications of the Pulse for decision makers.

What Does All of This Mean for Us?

Even though the research about how big trends can be seen by mining the data left behind by the world's Internet use is exciting, the purpose of this book will ultimately be about practical consequences. Businesses and governments can use this emerging science to their benefit—and not just to find better ways to promote products and ideas. Yes, that is included in the Pulse, but the social data revolution will have even more significant effects on society as a whole.

A good analogy for this might seem to be the impact e-business has had on business—but that may not be a close analogy at all. The effects of measuring the Pulse may be closer to how the adoption of common units of measure, laws, and language affected trade. The existence of these standards not only facilitated more trade and better trade but made new kinds of trade possible. In a similar vein, flying at night and sharing the air with thousands of other aircraft going different directions would not merely be less efficient without real-time data from instruments and radar; it wouldn't be *possible* at all. Microscopes didn't just make it easier to see small things; they made possible microbiology and, ultimately, most of modern medicine.

The Pulse will be similarly impactful. Businesses and governments won't just make faster and more accurate decisions by tracking big-picture trends in real time with these tools. They will do things completely differently. Information from the Pulse will become part of models that are dynamically simulating and forecasting businesses and the consequences of management decisions. Perhaps the furthest reaching effects of the Pulse will be beyond what we can imagine at this point. Even so, it will have at least the following four types of impact:

1. *Decisions based on responses to macro-trends will be faster.* We won't have to wait weeks—and certainly not 15 months as in the NBER report on the end of the recession—for indications of changes in fundamental economic factors, health conditions, and public opinions.
2. *In some cases, the Pulse will be more accurate than traditional methods of collecting data about major trends.* While the traditional methods like polls will continue to be used to calibrate and validate the Pulse, the Pulse will avoid some problems that plague traditional surveys.
3. *Trends that otherwise would not have been seen at all will be visible.* Traditional surveys have to be purpose-built. In other words, we have to have an idea of what we are looking for in advance, and then we have to collect that specific data. The Pulse offers a way to see trends that no one even knew to look for when the data was generated.

4. *Basic models of society will change.* Our ability to investigate and re-spond to the environment more quickly and accurately has implications for organizational structure, logistics, finance, and virtually every other part of business, government, and the study of humanity. This may be the greatest impact of the Pulse.

What economic benefits will the Pulse eventually help us realize? Our only benchmarks for this kind of fundamental shift are things like mass production, powered transportation, electricity, telecommunications, and computing. These innovations combined to revolutionize agriculture, health, life spans, per capita incomes, and even human rights. Our economy has grown by more than a factor of 100 since the start of these changes to society. The benefits of the Pulse are wide open.

Now, in the next three chapters, let's see how we got here and what "here" looks like. Chapter 2 puts tracking the big picture in context by showing a history—both recent and ancient—about how civilization has tried to ascertain the big picture and how that knowledge changed things. We review the history of how the trends would be approximated with traditional surveys and how early information technology had an impact.

Chapter 3 explains the birth of the digital Pulse—how several disciplines converged with a vast and rapidly expanding body of data from Internet users. We review not just how the number of connected people is growing but how much more they do in the Internet, how much more diverse the connected population is becoming, and how influential the "connected" are in society. We outline some of the major developments in the Pulse.

Chapter 4, the last chapter of Part I, will describe some of the relevant structure of the Internet as it applies to the Pulse. The Pulse relies on a system of incentives for individuals providing data to services and services making some of this data public. The basic methods used by developers to mine data and how this data is distributed around the Internet are discussed.

Notes

1. University of Michigan Ann Arbor Survey Research Center, as stated in a 2002 National Science Foundation grant proposal, "Identifying Causal Mechanisms Underlying Nonignorable Unit Nonresponse through Refusals to Surveys."
2. E. Morozov. *The Net Delusion: The Dark Side of Internet Freedom*, PublicAffairs, 2011

CHAPTER 2

The History of Seeing the Forest through the Trees

The enormous range and simultaneity of the wind-changes, testifying to the remarkable mobility of the air, were exceedingly conspicuous.
>—Sir Francis Galton (1861) on his early attempts to map large-scale weather patterns using weather stations and telegraph communications.

The most reliable way to forecast the future is to try to understand the present.
>—John Naisbitt, *Megatrends* (1982)

The evolution of methods we use to measure our society at a macro-level is one way to divide the history of civilization into useful periods. Instead of classification by the materials used (stone, bronze, and iron), we could define periods by what we measured about civilization, how we measured it, and why. After all, from the earliest kings to modern times, people have been trying to get a handle on things—to get the big picture, to see the forest through the trees.

As with any historical analysis, the point of this kind of retrospective is ultimately to tell us something not just about the past but also about the present and even the future. In this case, an examination of the history of assessing macro-trends itself reveals another macro-trend. As we found more sophisticated ways to measure more things about the big trends in society, the development of society itself accelerated. Motivations for collecting social data would drive methods, new methods would make new objectives for measurement possible, and motivations behind measurements, in turn, would become more ambitious. By enabling more responsive decisions, societies and economies could grow faster.

All such classifications are a bit arbitrary, but, prior to the Pulse, there are some clearly distinguishable periods according to the social metrics classification system of history: the tax and land surveys of kings, the dawn of statistics, and the age of computers. Then we can finish this chapter by discussing the challenges of the social sciences prior to the Pulse.

The King's Surveys

Money has been a key motivation for measurements in society and *of* society since the earliest days of civilization. A king collecting taxes had a good reason to find out how many subjects he had and what assets his subjects possessed. Whatever was to be taxed would be counted. Often, that meant that the king's surveyors would try to count not just every person but also every cow, goat, dwelling, or wagon. Military planning was another good reason to count people and things. A king had to know how large an army could be raised and how well supplied and equipped it could be. Money and power drove the ancient Egyptians, Romans, Chinese—and virtually every civilization since—to want to get the big picture assessments of their society.

From antiquity through the Renaissance, the method of data collection was simple in principle but sometimes monumental in execution. A legion of surveyors would be formed, and each would be in charge of counting different areas of the kingdom. Ideally, the surveyors would attempt to count every last person, cottage, wagon, or cow by visual identification. But often they would rely on the word of heads of households. The identification of individuals depended on name and location since, of course, nobody had anything like a social security number. This meant that counting efforts had to be coordinated so that two different surveyors didn't count the same person. Still, no doubt, double counting did happen just as certainly as the surveyors missed some people. And if a king's subjects suspected they would be taxed on, say, livestock, then they would have an incentive to sell, butcher, or hide at least some of the livestock before the census taker . arrived.

If people moved anytime during the long period it took to complete the census, it would be harder to count them. Fortunately for the surveyors, people moved a lot less before the availability of modern transportation. Unfortunately, a major survey could take years to complete, and it was still possible for significant migrations to occur in those time periods. Allegedly, some survey methods actually required mass migrations, as in the biblical account of the census edict of a governor of a large region of the Roman Empire. According to this account, all persons within the territory were ordered to return to their place of birth for counting. Yet the sheer logistics of doing so, the impossibility of verifying where anyone was actually born, and the apparent lack of practical motivation for such a feat would make such methods rare if not entirely impossible. (Why would the place of birth be relevant for taxes?)

The first attempt at a (mostly) comprehensive survey of the people of Britain was the great Domesday Book. As related in the early historical work *Anglo-Saxon Chronicles*, the purpose of the Domesday Book was to determine "How many hundreds of hides were in the shire, what land the king himself had, and what stock upon the land; or, what dues he ought to have by the year from the shire." This project took years to complete, and even then large population centers like London were excluded. The survey was planned in 1085, begun in 1086, and recorded into the book itself no earlier than 1087, when William I's son, William II, took over the reign of England. Given the differences in technologies for communication, travel, and data compilation, this endeavor must have seemed every bit as daunting as the modern U.S. decennial census.

It would be over 200 years after the Domesday project before a significantly more ambitious and detailed data collection effort would be attempted in Europe. In 1348, Giovanni Villani began to compile his comprehensive history of Florence, the *Nuova Cronica*. After Giovanni's death, his brother completed this monumental work, which included extensive statistics about the city. The Villanis gathered all of the traditional numbers of interest to kings for centuries: The population was about 94,000, about 25,000 of which were adult males that could bear arms, and so forth. In addition, the Villanis gathered other descriptive data earlier surveys had not tried to collect, such as the city's rate of consumption of several goods: 13,200 bushels of grain per week and 30,000 pigs per year, for example. The numbers of banks, physicians, bakeries, noblemen, foreign travelers, and schoolchildren were detailed. The Villanis collected data on the spread of the Black Plague (from which Giovanni himself died), and they noticed the curiously larger number of male infants compared to female infants. (In modern times, when a significant imbalance in the proportion of male to female births is noted, the cause is generally suspected to be infanticide, since the imbalance tends to favor whatever gender is preferred in that culture.)

Giovanni Villani was an exception among the people of his time. He saw detailed quantitative data as a way to describe Florence for the purpose of recording its historical significance. In almost all other cases for many millennia, taxes and the military were the sole purpose of a census. Yet, like the earlier surveys, a direct physical count was the only method of analysis available to the Villanis. The surveys were enormously expensive, and—until *Nuova Cronica*—only the most basic and relatively stable factors would be measured. Usually, nothing more dynamic than population counts and land could possibly be tracked. Measuring more fleeting, large-scale phenomena, such as the outbreak of a disease or a storm front, would be impossible. However, by the end of the eighteenth century, both the objectives and the methods of measuring society finally began to expand.

The Dawn of Stats, Theme-Maps, and Telegraphs

By the beginning of the nineteenth century, a convergence of new concepts and technologies would begin to improve what had not changed much for many millennia. The practice of finding the big picture about a society would be empowered by the emergence and combination of three ideas: a broader use of statistics, more advanced cartography (mapmaking), and improvements in rapid communication. Certainly, statistics and cartography emerged much earlier than the nineteenth century—but their continued evolution and wider adoption were reaching a critical mass. By the time telegraphy was widely adopted in the mid-19th century, these three ideas combined in a way that not only changed the cost and speed of existing macroscopic measures of society but also made practical new big pictures that would not have been possible earlier. In this period, for the first time, states or even curious academics could begin to track a disease outbreak as it occurred or map weather patterns the same day they formed.

In modern times, we tend to think of statistics as applying to marketing research, scientific experiments, economics, quality control, and virtually anything else that requires a quantitative measurement. Originally, however, the word had a much narrower use. The term "statistics" was introduced by the philosopher, economist, and legal expert Gottfried Achenwall in 1749. Achenwall derived the word from the Latin *statisticum*, meaning "pertaining to the state."

In other words, statistics was literally *the quantitative study of the state*. However, the power of the methods used in statistics would make it applicable to many more problems and usable by many other than officials of the state. Businesses and academics would find value in using these tools for purposes well beyond the traditional use of the census.

The methods of statistics would come, in part, from an esoteric field of mathematics that attracted some of the greatest thinkers of the time. What we now call "probability theory" was first developed in the sixteenth century by a talented Italian mathematician who also happened to have a gambling problem. Gerolamo Cardano was persistently in debt because of his gambling, and it is no surprise that his primary application of probability theory was to games of chance.

Even though he had a reputation for always being short of money, Cardano still had a significant intellectual stature. His reputation was such that once he introduced the idea of probability theory, other thinkers would be sure to follow. Later mathematicians began to find practical applications outside of gambling. By the seventeenth and eighteenth centuries, it was discovered that probability theory had implications for observations in general, and it became a powerful tool for scientific observation.

One of the great revelations of statistical inferences was that you didn't actually have to survey *everyone* to estimate something like the average number of children in a household, the average annual yield of farmers, or the distribution of ages of the population. You could just randomly select some subset of the population being measured and apply the survey questions to that smaller group.

The powerful tools of probability theory could then be used to make all sorts of inferences and estimates without direct observation. If you randomly selected 100 households in, say, London and found that 25 contained a newborn, you could use the tools of statistics to compute a "90% confidence interval" for the percentage of households with newborns of 18% to 32%. That is, there is a 90% chance that the actual share of the entire population with infants in their household is somewhere between 18% and 32%. The tools of statistics tell us that if half of households had infants, it would be extraordinarily unlikely to find only 25 such households out of a random sample of 100. Likewise, if only 1 in 10 households had an infant in the entire population, there is almost no chance that 100 randomly selected households would yield 25 households with an infant. You could sample more if you wanted a narrower range, but you certainly didn't have to have a complete census to reasonably estimate the number.

With statistical inferences, it is possible to measure things that otherwise would not have been feasible to measure at all. If you wanted to estimate the birth rate in your country, it would not be feasible to conduct a census of every household every year. Yet a relatively small random sample makes a moderately good estimate feasible even if you wanted to perform such a survey every year.

The emerging sophistication of cartography provided a way to present this new statistical data that made patterns much more intuitive. By the end of the eighteenth century, measuring distances and coordinates on land was becoming so sophisticated that it was possible to estimate the circumference of Earth very precisely merely by measuring Earth's curvature from the north to the south of France. (This, in fact, was the basis for the definition of the "meter"—one 10-millionth of the distance between the equator and either pole.) Even still, the precision of the maps was not the key revolution for big-picture trend-spotting. The big idea was simply that maps could be used for displaying information *other* than the shapes and distances of landmasses and borders. Maps could also be used to present population data, economic data, or even data about public health or weather patterns.

The discipline of the visualization of data on maps was called *thematic cartography*, and it provided a new way to get a big-picture view of what was really happening. Maps with themes about the tides, population distribution, or even the spread of diseases made big patterns immediately obvious to the human eye.

One early example of thematic cartography saved untold lives. A map of the spread of a disease showed the true cause behind the outbreak and made the solution clear to anyone who looked at the data. In the mid-nineteenth century, London had a densely packed population of 2.5 million people living without a modern infrastructure for water and waste disposal. Cholera outbreaks had visited the city every few years, killing thousands each time. In 1854, the disease appeared suddenly and with devastating effect in the Broad Street neighborhood of London. Only a week after the first observed case of cholera, one in ten residents of the neighborhood were dead from the disease.

The best explanation the health authorities of the time had for cholera was "bad air." Public health policy actually attempted to combat cholera by trying to reduce the stench in affected areas (e.g., emptying cisterns). Yet one physician, Dr. John Snow, thought cholera might be a waterborne illness, not an airborne one. He had made multiple unsuccessful attempts to convince health authorities of his theory. He had collected a lot of convincing data, but the patterns were not obvious when the information was shown in large tables of numbers.

Then Snow hit on the idea of creating a thematic map of the cholera outbreak. He used a street map that had a black bar for each address where someone had contracted the disease. The length of the bar indicated how many victims of cholera resided at that location. The map showed that cases tended to cluster near a particular well. (See Exhibit 2.1.)

The pattern was so strikingly obvious that it convinced local leaders to remove the handle from the pump at that well. Because the source of cholera was now known, this outbreak became the *last* major occurrence of cholera in London. For this and subsequent research, Snow became known as the first epidemiologist (a person who studies health at the level of the population).

Just under a decade after Snow's amazingly successful application of this new method of communicating data, the use of an emerging and practically instantaneous form of communication over long distances would make it possible to create thematic maps of patterns as fleeting as storm fronts. Sir Francis Galton employed the power of the newly expanding telegraph system to quickly assemble data from weather stations spread over Britain and parts of Europe. Galton, a cousin of Charles Darwin, also had the dubious distinction of being the founder of eugenics (the supposed improvement of the human species through selective breeding). Although today he might be more widely known for his contributions for eugenics, at the time, he was an esteemed mathematician, inventor, and explorer.

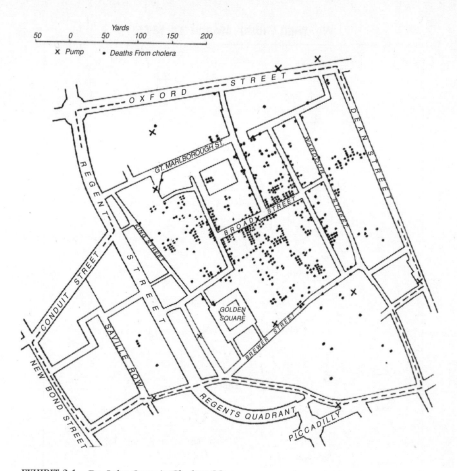

EXHIBIT 2.1   Dr. John Snow's Cholera Map

Broad Street Neighborhood of London, 1854 (one section magnified to show black bars indicating number of victims)

When Galton plotted this data on a map, it was possible, for the first time, to see entire storm fronts. Galton began his efforts to collect weather data from stations throughout Britain in 1861 by collecting data for every day in the month of December. At first, he published his weather maps for a mostly academic audience, but by 1875, Galton's weather maps were published in the *Times*. (See Exhibit 2.2.)

This weather map was printed in April 1, 1875, but it shows the weather patterns for the day before. This doesn't exactly meet our current definition of "real time," but we shouldn't underestimate the impact this kind of image must have had. We now take such maps for granted, but imagine if

WEATHER CHART, MARCH 31, 1875.

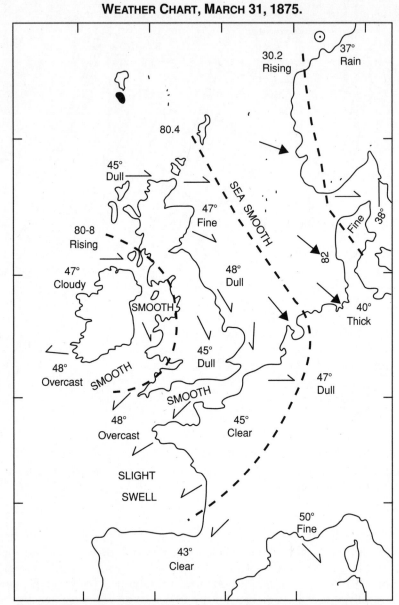

The dotted lines indicate the gradations of barometric pressure. The variations of the temperature are marked by figures, the state of the sea and sky by descriptive words, and the direction of the wind by arrows–barbed and feathered according to its force.

EXHIBIT 2.2   Francis Galton's First Weather Map to Be Published in the *Times*

Data from weather stations reported by telegraph for publication the following day you had never seen or even conceived of one before. Until Galton's time, weather was a phenomenon too big for one observer to fully visualize on a macroscopic scale. Just seeing that weather had *patterns* that were so large and moved so quickly over such great distances must have caused people to think of weather in an entirely new way.

Electromechanical communications like the telegraph had other implications for tracking big trends when they were applied to the financial markets. From the nineteenth century to as late as the 1970s, the "ticker tape" was the predominant method for tracking what was happening in financial markets. That slender paper tape with printed information on market prices was a real-time Pulse in its own right.

Galton's other contributions bring us full circle in this age of stats, maps, and telegraphs. Not only did he make use of cartography and telegraph-based communication in innovative ways, he was an innovator in the field of statistics and an influential figure behind some of the most basic and powerful ideas behind applied statistics. Galton's student, eventual biographer and overall booster Karl Pearson, developed several of these ideas further to create what we now call "mathematical statistics."

By the time World War II erupted, other mathematical luminaries such as Ronald A. Fischer had further developed statistics to be what we recognize today. Now every proper scientific study of any kind uses the statistical inference methods developed—almost entirely—prior to the war and prior to computers. Confidence intervals, for example (e.g., the 90% CI introduced earlier), were part of the intellectual offspring of this period. In fact, with few exceptions, the only significant improvements on scientific method since this time were not the basic mathematical procedures themselves but the sophistication of measurement instruments and the ability to perform vast calculations.

The Rise of the Machines

While the statistical methods used in scientific observation have not changed much since before World War II, the technology for applying those methods to huge sets of data evolved quickly. Computers changed virtually every area of research, and social science was no exception. It would be possible to use computers to quickly and cheaply analyze responses in surveys or pieces of financial data by the thousands or millions.

Of course, we don't *really* need a computer for some kinds of tasks, but other tasks would be utterly infeasible without computers. In the former case, if you have access to large pools of clerical labor, you could do this analysis the hard way. In World War II, for example, the Allies used a method they called "content analysis"—the study of recorded communications—as a method of military intelligence. It was common in military intelligence to analyze large numbers of military communications, but in one case the Allies applied content analysis to a public media. While they were not able to poll people in Germany or Japan, they could somehow get their hands on large numbers of local newspapers. (You may remember newspapers—they were sort of like blogs written by professionals but printed on paper and delivered to your door each morning).

Mass production–style, scores of clerical staff would read thousands of local papers to see the big trends. Town newspapers would list obituaries of local boys killed in action or promoted. The paper would report on a new factory being built and social events involving soldiers. None of these news items individually revealed classified information. Still, by totaling all of these individual micro-level reports of casualties, intelligence analysts could construct a macro-level report. This data combined to paint a picture of total casualties, troop movements, logistics shortages, and—ultimately—strategy. Content analysis could be applied to any records researchers could get access to in large enough quantities. For the clerks, the job was a fairly mechanical procedure; often they were instructed just to categorize content by keywords. In some ways, the procedure was similar to modern "sentiment analysis." When electronic, textual communications between individuals (emails, texts, blogs, etc.) came into wide use, the same methods could be applied in an automated way with the advantage of having much larger data sets analyzed much faster.

During World War II, computers using electromechanical relays usually were not used for text analysis. Instead, they were mostly used for numerical calculations—artillery firing tables, simulations of neutron interactions in the design of the atom bomb, and so on. But after the war, one of the earliest applications of the new vacuum tube–based computers was the U.S. Census. In fact, in 1951, the U.S. Census Bureau was the first to buy the new UNIVAC I—a computer bigger than your car and with *80,000 times less memory* than a postage-stamp-size iPod Nano. The influence of computing on painting the big picture was just beginning.

In almost every advance in computing, there was a parallel advance in the sophistication and ambitiousness of scale of measurements of the population and their activities. Computers had completely replaced ticker tapes for tracking prices of the market by the 1970's. Market research and political polls were becoming ubiquitous. A.C. Nielsen rating services, Gallup polls, and the Michigan Consumer Sentiment Index, among many others, either began or grew significantly during the earliest days of corporate computing. Health surveys were collecting data on birth rates, infant mortality, diseases, and death rates and compiling this data at a national level—eventually, for every nation. Economic research could produce much more detailed information about the state of a nation's economy than ever before.

Software that supports statistical analysis grew along with the hardware. In the 1960s, the earliest days of corporate use of computers, software firms like SAS and SPSS developed powerful systems for statistical analysis of large amounts of data. Today, many products help businesses track, analyze, and even predict the state of their business and their environment. Previously mentioned products such as business intelligence and predictive analytics have been developed by major business software players like IBM, Oracle, SAS, and a growing list of smaller competitors. "Dashboard" software tools are meant to be real-time or nearly real-time representations of the state of the organization. An executive using these tools might see if certain products are becoming more or less successful, if there are growing problems at some stores, or if a portfolio of projects is on track.

These important tools assist in the analysis of the business, but, as mentioned in Chapter 1, these tools should not be confused with the Pulse. These tools have, almost without exception, been entirely inward-looking. It is as if "military intelligence" meant merely keeping track of your own troops without looking at what the other side is doing. Or more like driving a car by keeping your head under the hood and watching the engine. Yes, executives can learn a lot about their business that way, but the big threats and opportunities on the horizon probably are not hidden in their existing databases.

We've covered about 5,000 years in very short order. A summary of this timeline is shown in Exhibit 2.3. Now we turn to a parallel history: the measurement challenges of social science.

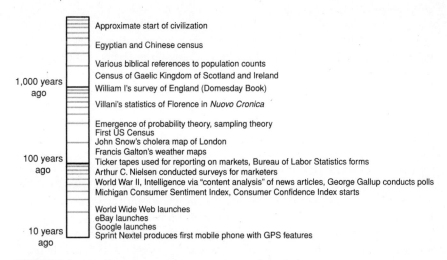

EXHIBIT 2.3 Timeline Prior to the Appearance of the Pulse

The Struggle to Become a Science

The study of society and even attempts to predict what might happen in a society are supposed to be what "social science" is all about. The term "social science" was coined during the French Revolution and has since come to broadly cover such diverse fields as anthropology, economics, psychology, history, and political science.

Yet, how much of a science social science is or can ever become is a matter of some debate. Justifiably or not, social science is often considered by many "true" scientists to be an oxymoron. I even know a few social scientists who not only concede this point but take some pride in it. Some believe, after all, that the really important issues about the world (i.e., social issues) are simply unquantifiable and beyond the tools of measurement used in the physical sciences. (Since the title of my first book was *How to Measure Anything*, you can imagine that I disagree.) In fact, in 2010, the American Anthropological Association (AAA) even decided to officially remove the word "science" from its mission statement altogether.[1] This did not reflect the views of many members and many of them strongly denounced this decision.

Now, there are certainly many instances of solid scientific inquiry happening in diverse parts of social science. Experimental psychology, economics, and other fields have frequently used methods that Pearson and Fisher would have considered mathematically sound. However, in other areas of the social sciences, some believe this separation from the standards of other sciences is a source of continued dilution of academic standards. One famous hoax revealed this lack of intellectual rigor in some fashionable areas of social science.

In 1996, a physicist named Alan Sokal submitted an article for publication in *Social Text*, which describes itself as a "postmodern cultural studies journal." The article was ostensibly about quantum theory, but Sokal deliberately wrote it to be complete nonsense. He titled his article "Transgressing the Boundaries: Toward a Transformative Hermeneutics of Quantum Gravity," and it included outrageously nonsensical statements like "In quantum gravity, as we shall see, the space-time manifold ceases to exist as an objective physical reality; geometry becomes relational and contextual; and the foundational conceptual categories of prior science—among them, existence itself—become problematized and relativized." The hoax worked; *Social Text* published the article.[2] This famous hoax serves to demonstrate how not only unscientific but virtually meaningless claims can be published in a peer-reviewed journal in some areas of academia.

The reputation of social science as being less quantitative than the physical sciences is actually a bit ironic, given the history of the field. Methods of making statistical inferences first arose in the development of mathematical methods *for the social sciences*—not the physical sciences. What some call the "hard" sciences (i.e., physics, chemistry, astronomy, etc.) must now meet rigorous statistical tests initially defined for social observations. Early hard scientists like Galileo certainly had none of these empirical tools at his disposal as he measured such things as the acceleration due to gravity or the period of a pendulum.

Some social sciences embraced formal mathematical models. As previously mentioned, mathematical sociology and CSS are steeped in mathematical theory and have been for decades. Among the phenomena analyzed are the nature and extent of personal relationships. Early research in this area showed, for example, that just about everyone on the planet can be connected to almost anyone else by fewer than 9 degrees of separation.[3] If Bob is your college buddy, who once worked with Darla, who took a ski class from John, who also taught Ahmed to ski, whose brother works for the minister of foreign affairs in Jordan, who personally knows the King of Jordan, then you are six degrees of separation from the King of Jordan, at most. I say "at most" because if there is a shorter route to the King of Jordan, then the degrees of separation would be a smaller number. The "six degrees of Kevin Bacon" game was a popular application of this otherwise abstract area of mathematics. The game involved selecting any random person involved in the movie industry and devising a series of six or fewer interpersonal connections to the actor Kevin Bacon. With just a few exceptions, that was the extent of the impact of CSS—a new parlor game.

Complex simulations of social networks did show interesting behaviors but, without more extensive empirical data, CSS would fall short of being a science. In an article in *Science* published in early 2009,[4] 15 different authors central to research in CSS lamented the obstacles to the growth of their field. The primary challenge was having a lot of theory and very little actual data. The authors noted that CSS is based on limited data sets gathered for the purpose of specific scientific studies. "To date, research on human interactions has relied mainly on one-time, self-reported data on relationships," the authors reported. However, they also foresaw changes: "The Internet offers an entirely different channel for understanding what people are saying, and how they are connecting."

Even when the social sciences have collected empirical data using traditional survey methods, there are problems with the data. Surveys based on self-reported behaviors (e.g., time spent socializing, time working, number of friends, etc.) are full of errors because people seem to have highly inaccurate memories of their own behaviors. Here are just a few problems:

- Imperfect recall has long been recognized as a problem in surveys, especially when it comes to personal relationships.[5] In 2005, a graduate student writing his PhD dissertation at the Massachusetts Institute of Technology used mobile phones to track physical locations and social interactions of students. The student showed that the social interactions other students self-reported on surveys had very little to do with their actual behavior.[6]

- Researchers have long known that what people report on surveys about their activities and what they actually do may not be the same things. In the analysis of preferences, researchers have two general methods at their disposal: stated and revealed preferences. A stated preference is what people may answer on a survey about, say, whether they prefer seeing movies to reading a book or going to the opera. A revealed preference, however, considers not how people answered a survey but how they actually choose to spend their time and their money. If you say you prefer the opera to movies but you haven't spent any money or time going to the opera for the last five years and you go to the movies every week, then your revealed and stated preferences are inconsistent. Researchers sometimes combine stated and revealed preferences,[7] although there is still discussion about the precise manner and narrow situations in which this can be done.[8]

- Researchers themselves sometimes alter the outcomes of their measurements by how they frame questions or even by subjects' knowledge that they are being observed in the first place. The Hawthorne Effect is named for a study in 1939 at the Hawthorne power plant in Illinois which demonstrated how much the knowledge of being watched affects behavior. Researchers attempting to study productivity and how it correlates to working conditions (light levels, temperature, etc.). Yet no matter how researchers changed the environment, worker productivity improved because workers knew they were being watched. This effect has also been shown to be a significant factor in research regarding social relationships. More recently, the related "interviewer effect" is shown to be a significant source of error in social network research.[9]

- A 1993 study showed that a key measure of consumer confidence, the Michigan Consumer Sentiment Index (MCSI), was in a large part simply a reflection of what people heard on the news about the economy.[10] The study showed that 70% of the MCSI can be explained by other reported economic data. The MCSI, in other words, appears to be merely measuring reactions to media reports about the economy.

- Even some influential studies in the social sciences have relied on questionable methods. Two famous studies on sexuality, the *Hite Report* and the *Kinsey Reports*, each relied on thousands of interviews. The subjects generally were selected by referral, not randomized methods, and results of interviews were assessed qualitatively. In other studies, interviews of only a few individuals are qualitatively assessed.[11]

Still, even with all the problems mentioned above, the methods and tools used until now have gotten us pretty far in terms of tracking the world's big picture. Now, we turn to how the Pulse will be changing all of how we measure major trends in society.

Notes

1. N. Wade. "Anthropology a Science?," *New York Times*, December 9, 2010.
2. A. Sokal. "Transgressing the Boundaries: Toward a Transformative Hermeneutics of Quantum Gravity," *Social Text* #46/47, pp. 217–252 (spring/summer 1996).
3. S. Milgram. "The Small World Problem." *Psychology Today*, May 1967. pp 60–67.
4. D. Lazer et al. "Computational Social Science," *Science* 323, no. 5915 (2009): 721–723.
5. H.R. Bernard, P. Killworth, D. Kronenfeld, and L. Sailer. "The Problem of Informant Accuracy: The Validity of Retrospective Data." *Annual Review of Anthropology* 13 (2009), 495–517.
6. N. Eagle. *Machine Perception and Learning of Complex Social Systems*, PhD diss., Massachusetts Institute of Technology, Department of Media Arts and Sciences, 2005.
7. A. Christopher, J. Herriges, and C. Kling. "Combining Revealed and Stated Preferences: Consistency Tests and Their Interpretation," *American Journal of Agricultural Economics* 85, no. 3 (August 2003): 525–537.
8. J.-C. Huang, T.C. Habb, and J.C. Whitehead. "Willingness to Pay for Quality Improvements: Should Revealed and Stated Preference Data Be Combined?" *Journal of Environmental Economics and Management* 34, no. 3 (November 1997): 240–255; ww.sciencedirect.com/science/journal/00950696.
9. P.V. Marsden. "Interviewer Effects in Measuring Network Size Using a Single Name Generator." *Social Networks* 25 (2003): 1–16.
10. J.C. Fuhrer. "What Role Does Consumer Sentiment Play in the U.S. Macroeconomy?" *New England Economic Review* (January/February 1993): 32–44.
11. F. J. Roethlisberger and W. J. Dickson. *Management and the Worker* (Cambridge, MA: Harvard University Press, 1939).

CHAPTER 3

Emergence of the Pulse and the New Research Discipline

2009 will generate more data than all of human history to date.
—Andreas Weigen, former chief scientist of Amazon

The Internet has made measurable what was previously immeasurable.
—Dr. Gunther Eysenbach, epidemiologist
and inventor of Infodemiology

In the context of tracking macroscopic patterns of society, the Pulse is a very recent phenomenon. Only late in the first decade of the twenty-first century did we have sound scientific research based on sufficient quantities of our individual, publicly accessible digital footprints to see meaningful macro-patterns. What makes tracking the Pulse possible now is a combination of factors:

1. *The number and diversity of Internet users grows.* Depending on the source, anywhere from 70% to 80% of U.S. adults use the Internet. Even the developing world now has a higher percentage of Internet users in 2010 than the United States had in 1995. The fastest growth in Internet use is generally among groups that have used it the least so far. However, even the lack of uniformity that still persists is not an obstacle; it can even make Internet users more relevant for some measures.
2. *Each user spends more time in more activities on the Internet, and these activities are likely to leave publicly visible digital footprints in several useful ways.* The average Internet user in the United States spends about 13 hours a week online performing many activities that indicate something about health, the economy, social trends, and political opinions.
3. *There is growth in interest among researchers in developing new methods of using this data.* Just a few years ago, it would have been hard

33

getting published using such an unconventional data source. Very recent research, however, has been published in prestigious academic journals by prestigious institutions and respected scientists.

While these factors make the Pulse more feasible, there are still obstacles to overcome—although not technological or mathematical ones. The primary obstacle seems to be pervasive beliefs that cause some to be dismissive of research based on Internet usage even in the face of what should be scientifically convincing evidence. There are legitimate challenges, of course, and some concerns must be taken seriously. More often, however, objections to these powerful new tools are really no more than basic misconceptions about scientific research and statistical methods.

Ubiquitous Use of the Internet

Chapter 2 mentioned an article in the magazine *Science* in which 15 researchers acknowledged that the obstacle to computational social science becoming a mature science was the lack of data. Even still, within the past few years, more people have been doing more things that provide the data these researchers needed. If people were involved in the sorts of activities that leave publicly visible footprints on the Internet, then the sheer size of the Internet would make this new science the most data-rich science of them all. Of course, the Internet had been growing exponentially well before the *Science* article. Nearly one third of the people of the entire planet have Internet access, and by the end of 2010, about two-thirds had a mobile phone.

The Internet is one of those things that is so large that just measuring it is a difficult task. The sources of information about the growth of Internet users sometimes use methods similar to those described in the previous chapter: big surveys. The irony should not be lost. The case for the existence of and the need for the exploitation of the Pulse initially have to rely on at least some traditional measurement methods. At some point, perhaps, such traditional survey methods will be used primarily as a periodic validation and calibration of the Pulse. But, until then, traditional methods are the best way to determine how many people participate in the Internet and what they do with it.

There are many traditional, survey-based sources for the growth of the Internet, and they sometimes give greatly different numbers. The International Telecommunications Union (ITU; an agency of the United Nations), A.C. Nielsen, Forrester Research, Pew Research, the Harris Poll, IDC, and many other organizations attempt to estimate the number of Internet users and their activities both worldwide and by country. They conduct surveys ranging from a few hundred to tens of thousands of people, and they rely primarily on what people say when they answer the surveys. Other sources are a bit closer to the Pulse in that they collect data directly from users who have downloaded software that tracks their behavior. (Although, since these sources produce their reports only monthly and they are not otherwise publicly available, data collected in this manner is not quite the Pulse.)

At one point, I was going to undertake the task of aggregating these sources, but their number and the difficulty in comparing very different methods of measurement made doing so impractical. Fortunately, some sources already make it their mission to aggregate this same data. eMarketer, for example, reviews about 4,000 different sources on the usage of the Internet. Its staff understands how to compare sources that use different methods, and the company produces over 80 reports per year about a variety of online activities and trends. Where there are multiple sources, I'll leave the aggregation to eMarketer. I'll use other sources selectively when they appear to be the only source.

First, let's discuss overall growth in Internet use and then get into the qualitative details of that growth. The growth rate in Internet users world-wide is shown in Exhibit 3.1. The chart shows the number of Internet users with a range of optimistic and pessimistic estimates shown based on differences in data sources. The differences among the sources are relatively small and are very likely due to differences in collection methods. For example, a phone poll would exclude people who don't have phones; obviously, these people are also much less likely to be Internet users. Since these are random

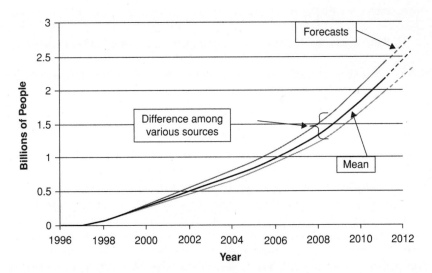

EXHIBIT 3.1   Growth in Number of Internet Users Worldwide

samples, there is always the possibility that random selection errors could explain some of the differences. Yet, because these surveys tend to include a few thousand people, random sampling error is much smaller than the differences shown.

In 2000, there were approximately 300 million Internet users worldwide, just under a sixth of what there were in 2010. Numbers going back before 2000 are less available and less reliable, especially for the developing world, but they do exist. According to IDC, in 1995, less than half of 1% of the world's population had Internet access. Including changes in the overall population, this comes to over a 100-fold increase in the last 15 years. Going back a little farther, there were just about 3 million Internet users worldwide in 1990. By 2010, there were almost 2 billion people connected to the Internet—about three out of every ten people in the world. Even taking conservative estimates, this is better than a 600-fold increase in the span of one generation. *In all of human history, perhaps no technology, idea, form of government, religion, language, plague, or empire has ever spread that fast to such a large share of the world.*

One measure of how accepted an idea has become is the point in time when people begin to see it not as a luxury or privilege but as a fundamental human right. Apparently Internet access has attained this status. A worldwide poll of 27,000 adults conducted by GlobeScan showed that 79% of the population thinks of Internet access as a fundamental human right. People who already have Internet access are more likely to think that way (87%), but even the majority of people without Internet access believe that getting it is their right (71%). And history tells us that once people see something as a fundamental right, they often end up getting it one way or the other.

If there is any doubt about continued growth, we need only consider the higher percentage of users among the young. It's no surprise that the most intensive users of the Internet are the youngest—over 90% of U.S. teenagers are connected. One study by the Internet security firm AVG showed that 82% of newborns in 10 Western countries now have an Internet presence. The United States holds the highest propensity to post baby pictures—92% of U.S. babies have a presence on the Internet before they can say "Google." Perhaps not all of these children will become avid Internet fans, but it seems likely that a child with early exposure will be an Internet user for life.

The growth in diversity of users and activities on the Internet has also been striking. While "Internet user" meant a relatively narrow demographic 20 years ago, it has spread across age, gender, race, national boundaries, and languages. There is still what some would call a "digital divide," (the difference in Internet access among social classes) but most measures indicate this gap is shrinking, even if only slowly in some areas. The general rule in the growth of Internet use has been this: *The lower a given group starts in*

Internet usage, the faster Internet use in that group grew. The narrowing of these gaps is useful for the Pulse. If we are going to use Internet activity as a measure and leading indicator of major trends, then it would be best if Internet use was at least somewhat representative across groups. Here are just a few examples of the narrowing gap in Internet access.

Narrowing the Gap: An Increasing Uniformity of Internet Access

- *Developed versus developing world gap.* The fastest growth in Internet use has been among groups and nations that have used the Internet the least (which is not that surprising since they had the most room to grow). According to the ITU, approximately one in five people in the developing world has Internet access.[1] Combining multiple reports, Exhibit 3.2 shows that while the developed world saw a growth of about 40% in Internet access from 2005 to 2010, the developing world had a growth of about 170%. This is still less than a third of the rate of Internet access of the developed world, but the gap has closed considerably. In 2005, a person in the developed world was 6.5 times as likely as a person in the developing world to have Internet access. In 2010, it was only 3.4 times as likely for a developed world person to have Internet access as developing world person.
- *Age gap.* Older people are less likely to use the Internet than younger ones, but they have also been closing the gap. Exhibit 3.3 shows that

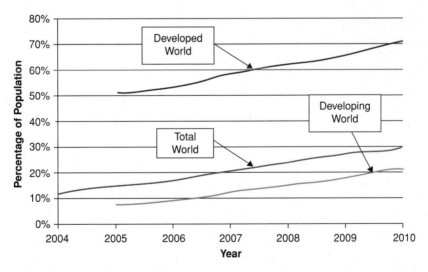

EXHIBIT 3.2 Developing World versus Developed World Growth in Internet Use
Source: ITU data.

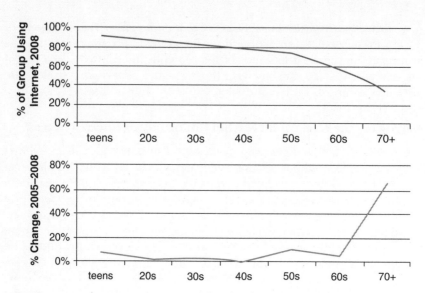

EXHIBIT 3.3   Internet Use and Growth by Age in the United States
Source: Derived from Pew Research data.

while older persons have the lowest chance of being online, that same crowd grew 66% from 2005 to 2008 while younger age groups all grew 10% or less.

- *Gender gap.* Prior to 2000, there was a significant but already narrowing gender gap.[2] Males were more likely to use the Internet than females and they spent more time on average online than females. According to eMarketer, the gap had disappeared by 2005 and since that time slightly more women than men are on the Internet.
- *Ethnic gap.* As with all other categories, the lower a group started out, the faster it grew. In the United States, African Americans, Hispanic Americans, and Native Americans still have less Internet access than Americans of European or Asian descent, but their usage also grew the fastest. According to the National Telecommunications and Information Administration—a part of the U.S. Department of Commerce—the former three groups had broadband access rates under 33% in 2007, but that figure had grown by more than a third by 2009. Most ethnic differences in Internet use in the United States shrink significantly when adjusted for differences in education, income, and employment status.
- *Income gap.* Income is still a strong factor in Internet access. However, the poorest people who had the lowest chance of being on the Internet also had the fastest growth. A Cornell University study showed that people who made over $75,000 per year were almost twice as likely

to have Internet access as those who made less than $25,000 per year. Curiously, the lower-income group spent over four hours per week more on the Internet than did the more affluent.[3]

There are still differences among groups. Income and education are the most significant factors in whether someone has Internet access. And some individual activities do vary among age categories. The young are much more likely to play games and less likely to search for health information online than older users. However, even though there is not a perfectly uniform representation of all groups, the knowledge of the differences among these groups is useful. If we are aware of these differences, we can adjust our measurements of the Pulse accordingly.

Furthermore, in some ways, the differences themselves are important for the purposes of the Pulse. When it comes to measuring and forecasting things like economic activity and social trends, a truly random sample is not necessarily the best one. For example, when estimating economic activity, it makes sense to look at people who generate the most economic activity. While Internet users are about 28% of the world's population, they easily make up the majority of the world's income. In the United States, Internet users are twice as likely as nonusers to make over $40,000 per year, and they are more than five times as likely to make over $75,000 per year.[4]

Internet users are also more socially connected. This might be a surprise to those who think of Internet users as more likely to be social hermits. In 2001, a survey of 2,500 randomly selected citizens of Great Britain showed that Internet users were more likely to belong to community groups or voluntary organizations than nonusers.[5] A 2009 Pew Research survey of 2,258 Americans showed that Internet users are 43% more likely to interact with their neighbors than nonusers. These are not just inconvenient differences for the statistician who wants a truly random sample of a population. They are differences that are actually more relevant for certain models of social activity and economic activity.

Digital Lives: Increasing Time and Activities per Person

Of course, the volume of the data would not be as interesting if only the number of users was growing. The time spent per user and the variety of things they do are growing—especially in activities which leave publicly available digital traces. According to the Harris Poll, the time spent per user on the Internet with a PC was growing steadily. Exhibit 3.4 shows that time spent on the Internet per person per week almost doubled in a decade to a total of 13 hours per week on average. Considering the fact that the number

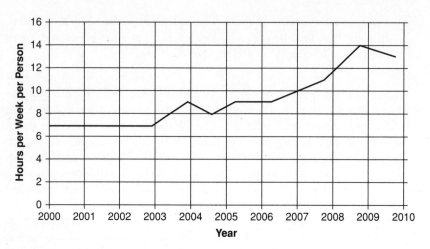

EXHIBIT 3.4   Average Time Spent on the Internet among Those with Internet Access

of users has grown by a factor of about six in ten years, the total of all time spent by all Internet users has increased by a factor of 12.

Curiously, while time spent online grew sharply from 2006 to 2008, this trend seems to have leveled off in 2009. Perhaps the Great Recession provides some economic reasons for this recent stagnation, but that can't be the whole story. As pointed out before, some research has shown that people in lower income brackets, while being less likely to have Internet access, are also known to use the Internet more often when they do have access. In fact, since people now are more likely to use the Internet to help in job searches, the unemployed may spend more time on the Internet. Another explanation proposed by some analysts was that average users are becoming savvier about their time on the Internet. They are more productive and spend less time searching for what they want. They have well-worn paths on the Internet and accomplish their business more quickly.

People do so many things on the Internet that we apparently needed new verbs to describe them. The fact that they perform so many of the "new verbs"—blog, tweet, friend, Google, and so on—means that we have not just a quantity but a variety of useful data. In contrast, when people spend time on tasks like online banking, they reveal almost no data to the public. We may only see how much traffic a bank's Web site gets in total, but not much other than that. Likewise, email and instant messaging are activities that generally don't leave publicly available traces—but those sorts of activities are not the ones that have grown the most.

The Pulse is concerned with the things that leave easily accessible digital traces. The tendency to engage in activities that leave publically available records is really what has changed the most since 2007. The Internet had been growing at a fantastic rate overall, but only recently have so many of the activities left so much freely available data for us to track. Here are the six areas of the Pulse I described in Chapter 1 and how activities in each area have grown.

Growth in the Six Key Areas of the Pulse

- *Surf*. Even though it doesn't take as much time as other activities, searching is the activity shared by the most Internet users (second only to email). According to Pew Research, 89% of all Internet users use the Internet to search for information. Google publically provides detailed search behavior data to those who bid on keywords in order to rank higher on searches. Now it has made some of that data available to the general public with Google Trends and Google Insights for Search. Correlating search terms on Google to economic trends and disease outbreaks has been one of the most active areas of research in the Pulse.
- *Friend* (the verb). By far, the fastest area of growth is in the use of the social media sites that allow people to manage connections with friends and colleagues. According to a report by the Nielsen Company, time spent on social media sites has grown by 82% from 2008 to 2009—from 3 to 5.5 hours per month. By comparison, the increase in total time spent in all activities on the Internet during that same period was only 27%. This means that social networking *alone* explains a majority of the growth in Internet use in that year. There are several social media sites, but the elephant in the room is the fantastically successful creation of Mark Zuckerberg, Facebook, which easily makes up the majority of all time spent in social media online. Depending on privacy settings, just about anything on Facebook could be available for public viewing.
- *Say*. An obvious example of one of the most explicit ways we leave digital footprints is blogging. There were already over 100 million blogs in the world by 2008. By 2009, the "micro-bloggers" of Twitter were creating 100 million tweets per month; by the end of 2010, there were over 2 billion tweets per month, or over 800 Tweets per second. According to eMarketer, there are about 26 million bloggers in the United States today, or about 8.5% of the U.S. population. Most bloggers want their posts to be viewed by anyone so this is a large amount of publicly available content for the Pulse. This is data the users simply volunteer without any solicitation from a researcher. The content is unstructured but can still be analyzed using computational methods that analyze such things as the "sentiment" of text.
- *Go*. More users share where they are. A report from Skyhook Wireless shows that by early 2010, there were already over 7,000 apps that

use Global Positioning System (GPS) locations of mobile phones. Most are iPhone apps, and 90% of them are free. Only a few of these apps provide both some publicly available clues about where crowds (not individuals) go and have a large enough user base to be useful as a source of the Pulse. Facebook launched its location-sharing mobile feature in 2010. An app named Yelp lets the user write and read location-based reviews of local businesses, and it might be possible to count these reviews as indicators of economic activity.

- *Buy.* More and more of what people buy, they buy online. According to the 2009 Pew Research survey, 71% of Internet users have made a purchase online—about half of Internet users did so in a given month. While we spend much less time online in this activity compared to other online activities, retail sales have grown steadily and now make up about 8% of all retail in the United States. For example, eBay, one of the largest online retailers, leaves a lot of data for everyone to see. Each auction is publicly visible, and even completed auctions are available for some period of time.

- *Play.* This is definitely the most nascent area of the Pulse. Some research shows that our moods, environments, and recent events can change our aversion to risks and, therefore, the strategies we use in games. There is currently no research correlating online game play to economic, social, or health trends, but it could become an important area of the Pulse. According to Pew Research, playing games is the number-one online activity for Internet users under the age of 18. And games have proven addictive for older Internet users as well. Facebook game apps like Farmville have become remarkably successful. Not all online game play currently generates data for the Pulse, but there is great potential. Even the ability to see the current number of players from multiple online games might say something about available leisure time.

So far in this chapter, I have presented data from various sources, which sometimes used traditional surveys to track Internet usage. I also mentioned some sources that use software volunteers must download so that their Internet use is monitored in detail. Both of these sources are proprietary data that the researchers release in monthly reports (not real time) and, as such, are not defined as part of the macroscopic Pulse. Fortunately, there are free, online sources for some of this information and one such source gave me access to some detailed historical information about Web site use.

To approximate where the most visited sites stand on total time spent relative to other sites, I used the near-real-time site rankings available on Alexa.com. Alexa.com is owned by Amazon, and it gathers statistics on thousands of Web sites. The source of this data comes from millions of end users who have downloaded an Alexa toolbar. This tool sends Alexa

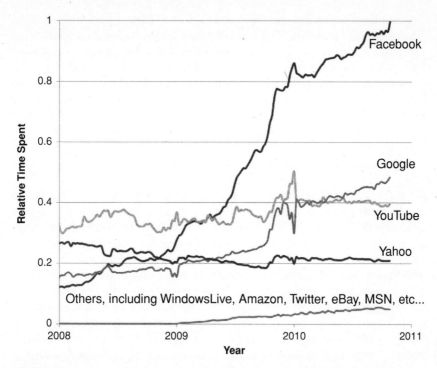

EXHIBIT 3.5 Relative Time Spent on Different Sites with Publicly Available Data
Source: Derived from Alexa.com data on user reach and average time spent per visitor per day.

information about what sites users are visiting. It collects where they went, how long they stayed, how many pages they visited, and so on. Unlike some similar sources, anyone can publically view online charts of this data. Executives at Alexa also indulged my request for detailed historical data provided in Excel spreadsheets.

I used Alexa's worldwide "reach" data, which indicates the percentage of all Internet users who visited the site, times the average amount of time per visitor. Multiple visits per day for a single visitor are all included in the time spent. Exhibit 3.5 shows weekly points from 2008 to 2010 for each of several popular Internet sites. (The data is updated daily but I retrieved only what I needed.) The chart shows results in relative terms where all are compared to the most time-intensive activity on the chart (which is set to a value of 1).

This data shows that, as of the end of 2010, Facebook is a clear winner when it comes to how we spend our time compared to the other sites on the chart. The other top sites garnered significantly less of our attention.

Even though Google was the number-one ranked site by number of visitors, users spent less than half as much time on Google. We just use Google to search, and then we go to the site we were really looking for. (Also note the curious symmetrical, opposing blips on Google and Youtube at the end of 2009.[6]) We spend so much more time on Facebook that you can't even see other popular sites like Twitter and eBay on this scale. The most recent points in this data show users spent 20 times as much time on Facebook as they spend on Twitter, 30 times as much as they spend on eBay, and 37 times as much as they spend on Amazon.

Nielsen has data on Internet activities as well, but it measures different things, and we cannot directly compare the Alexa.com data with Nielsen. The Nielsen Report combines different online services under categories like search, social media, or online auctions whereas the Alexa data is for specific sites, which may have more than one use. For example, the Nielsen Report shows that as of June 2010, we spent 6.5 times as much time on social media as in all search activities (Google, Yahoo!, etc.) combined. The Alexa method, on the other hand, shows that time spent on Google alone is almost half as much as time spent on Facebook. This is probably because people use Google for more than just search, not because of the added time spent in other social media (which is small compared to the amount of time spent on Facebook). Also, the term "social media" in the Nielsen Report includes Twitter. Although Twitter was originally billed as a micro-blogging site, the fact that you can have followers on Twitter also makes it a de facto social media site.

Nielsen also differs in the nature of its sampling. Alexa makes no attempt to recruit a random or representative sample whereas Nielsen controls the sample set closely. Considering these differences in how activities are categorized, the Alexa findings are not entirely inconsistent with those of Nielsen. The growth in Facebook, the major social media site, is clear in both sources.

Likewise, data from another major source of information about the Internet, comScore, shows the relative ranking of search engines Google and Yahoo! to be more or less consistent with Alexa.com. Again, comScore is looking at search activity alone, not other uses of these sites. And while Alexa advised potential users of this data that it was okay for relative comparisons, not absolute time measures, its data is fairly consistent with Nielsen's.

In later chapters, I show how more detailed data from traditional sources can be used to validate and calibrate data from the Pulse. Differences in how data is combined are taken into account, and a much larger set of points of comparison are used. With these considerations in mind, data from Alexa may be just as relevant as that from Nielsen and comScore. The Alexa data, however, may be more useful because we don't have to wait a month for each report.

Having this information updated daily instead of monthly could be critical if we are going to use Internet traffic, blogs, Google searches, and other online behaviors to forecast economics, health, politics, and more. Tracking a site's activity is important because the relative rankings of these sites could all change. The popularity of social media sites in particular has been volatile. The once-prominent Myspace has lost its lead even among the young, where it focuses. According to the Alexa method, the total time spent on Facebook by the end of 2010 is 100 times as much as total time spent on Myspace. The Myspace share of social media time has been hit so hard, the company has decided that it will no longer even call itself a social media site.[7] What is clear is that social media, in some form or another, is here to stay.

Open Pastures: A New Field of Research

With only a few exceptions, all of the academic research focused on exploiting Internet data to track and forecast real-world events has been published after 2008. Since that time, popular media outlets and peer-reviewed publications alike presented research showing that the traces we leave about our daily activities on the Internet do correlate with unemployment, foreclosures, political opinions, customer sentiment, and even the outbreaks of flu viruses. And researchers are realizing that they are just barely scratching the surface.

The timeline in Exhibit 3.6 shows that prior to 2009, social research based on data available on the Internet was very sparse except for some seminal work. Then several articles appearing in 2009 showed how the frequency of Internet search on particular key words predict real-world events. Most notably, an article published in *Nature* in early 2009 showed how influenza can be traced with Google searches, no doubt giving some needed scientific credibility to the idea of using Internet data as a valid research tool. Note that almost all of the research before 2010 was related to correlating search volumes (from either Yahoo! or Google) to other trends. In 2010, new research was also looking at Twitter and location sharing as sources of information for the Pulse.

A particularly noteworthy point on this chart is the year 2006. This is when Facebook and Twitter became available as well as Google Trends (the tool that gives public access to search volume history for particular search terms). These three represent a significant part of the data used in the Pulse. They were also the inspiration and source for many subsequent studies about the use of social data available from the Internet.

Absent from this chart are areas of research that were not based on data from the Internet, even though large quantities of at least some of

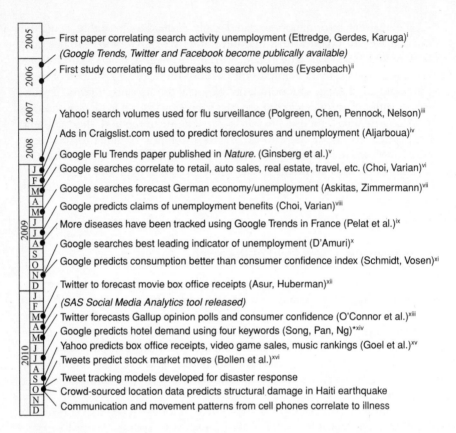

2005 ● First paper correlating search activity unemployment (Ettredge, Gerdes, Karuga)[i]
(Google Trends, Twitter and Facebook become publically available)

2006 ● First study correlating flu outbreaks to search volumes (Eysenbach)[ii]

2007 Yahoo! search volumes used for flu surveillance (Polgreen, Chen, Pennock, Nelson)[iii]

Ads in Craigslist.com used to predict foreclosures and unemployment (Aljarboua)[iv]

2008 Google Flu Trends paper published in *Nature*. (Ginsberg et al.)[v]

2009
J ● Google searches correlate to retail, auto sales, real estate, travel, etc. (Choi, Varian)[vi]
F
M ● Google searches forecast German economy/unemployment (Askitas, Zimmermann)[vii]
A
M ● Google predicts claims of unemployment benefits (Choi, Varian)[viii]
J ● More diseases have been tracked using Google Trends in France (Pelat et al.)[ix]
J
A ● Google searches best leading indicator of unemployment (D'Amuri)[x]
S
O ● Google predicts consumption better than consumer confidence index (Schmidt, Vosen)[xi]
N
D Twitter to forecast movie box office receipts (Asur, Huberman)[xii]

2010
J
F *(SAS Social Media Analytics tool released)*
M ● Twitter forecasts Gallup opinion polls and consumer confidence (O'Connor et al.)[xiii]
A ● Google predicts hotel demand using four keywords (Song, Pan, Ng)*[xiv]
M
J ● Yahoo predicts box office receipts, video game sales, music rankings (Goel et al.)[xv]
J ● Tweets predict stock market moves (Bollen et al.)[xvi]
A
S Tweet tracking models developed for disaster response
O ● Crowd-sourced location data predicts structural damage in Haiti earthquake
N Communication and movement patterns from cell phones correlate to illness
D

[i]"Using Web-Based Search Data to Predict Macroeconomic Statistics," *Communications of the ACM*, November 2005. [ii]"Infodemiology: Tracking Flu-Related Searches on the Web for Syndromic Surveillance," *AMIA 2006 Symposium Proceedings* 2006 (2006): 244–248. [iii]"Using Internet Searches for Influenza Surveillance," *Oxford Journals* 47, no. 11 (2008): 1443–1448. [iv]"Craigslist & the Economy: Predicting Unemployment and Foreclosure Trends from Online Classified Advertisements," *The Connexions Project* m19512 (2009): 1–2. [v]J. Ginsberg, M. H. Mohebbi, R. S. Patel, L. Brammer, M. S. Smolinski, and L. Brilliant. "Detecting Influenza Epidemics Using Search Engine Query Data," *Nature* 457 (2009):1012–1014. [vi]"Predicting the Present with Google Trends," *Google Research* April 10 (2009). [vii]"Google Econometrics and Unemployment Forecasting," *IZA Discussion Papers* June, no. 4201 (2009). [viii]"Predicting Initial Claims for Unemployment Benefits," Google Inc, July 5, 2009. [ix]C. Pelat, C. Turbelin, A. Bar-Hen, A. Flahault, and A. Valleron. "More Diseases Tracked by Using Google Trends," *Emerging Infectious Diseases* 15, no. 8 (2009):1327–1328. [x]"Predicting Unemployment in Short Samples with Internet Job Search Query Data," *Bank of Italy – Research Department* 18403 (2009):1–17. [xi]"Forecasting Private Consumption: Survey-Based Indicators vs. Google Trends," *Ruhr Economic Papers* 155 (2009):1–23. [xii]"Predicting the Future with Social Media," *Cornell University Library* arXiv:1003.5699v1 (2010):1–8. [xiii]B. O'Connor, R. Balasubramanyan, B. R. Routledge, and N. A. Smith. "From Tweets to Polls: Linking Text Sentiment to Public Opinion Time Series," *School of Computer Science Carnegie Mellon University* May (2010). [xiv]"Forecasting Demand For Hotel Rooms With Search Engine Query Volume Data," *School of Hotel and Tourism Management* (2010):1–24. [xv]S. Goel, J. M. Hofman, S. Lahaie, D. M. Pennock, and D. J. Watts. "Predicting Consumer Behavior with Web Search," *PNAS* Early Edition (2010):1–5. [xvi]Johan Bollen, Huina Mao, and Xiao-Jun Zeng. "Twitter Mood Predicts the Stock Market," *Cornell University* arXiv:1010.3003v1, no. 14 October (2010):1–8.

EXHIBIT 3.6   Pulse Academic Research Timeline

the needed data may already be available online. Most notably, Nicholas Christakis of the Harvard Medical Center and James Fowler of the University of California–San Diego have completed several studies showing how social networks can predict not only outbreaks of infectious disease but also the spread of alcoholism, emotions, and depression. They applied computational social science methods to model outbreaks of diseases and emotions, but the data was gathered specifically for their studies, not from a social media source like Facebook (still, the potential of this research merits a dedicated chapter in this book).

Exhibit 3.6 only shows studies published prior to November 2010 showing predictive effectiveness of Internet behavior. Much more research on this topic had already started as this book was going to print. To keep up with a rapidly moving field as it becomes available, I will post the most significant new research on this book's Web site at www.pulsethenewscience.com. The research mentioned above will be covered in more detail in Chapters 5 through 8.

Proving the Pulse: Addressing Misconceptions about the Data

The researchers mentioned earlier will be the first to tell you that we can't take the correlation between online behaviors and real-world trends for granted. They must be rigorously tested and based on convincing empirical evidence. Still, there are common objections to using this kind of data to predict human events, and these objections are based on misconceptions about the nature of scientific method. Even qualified researchers sometimes have succumbed to these fallacies.

I use the term "correlation" a lot in this book so it might be helpful to review this basic concept. A correlation is a value between −1 and 1 that shows how well one set of data "fits" another set. Suppose I plotted the heights of people versus their shoe size. I would probably find that very tall people also have larger-than-average feet and that short people usually have smaller feet. There will, of course, be exceptions, but that simply means that these two sets of numbers (height and shoe size) are not perfectly correlated. A correlation of zero means that the two values are unrelated (e.g., the last two digits of your social security and your shoe size). A negative correlation means that as one value increases, the other decreases (e.g., cholesterol and your chance of living to 90, education and years in prison, etc.)

In our discussion, we often show how well a model predicts something that changes over time. This could be illnesses, wages, inflation, presidential approval ratings, or many other things. We could show how well a model predicts something by plotting it on a timeline, as we show on the right side of Exhibit 3.7. If we see the two different values move up and down very

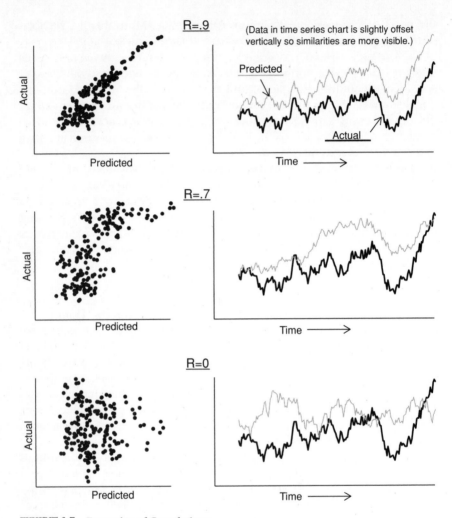

EXHIBIT 3.7   Examples of Correlations

closely together, we call them correlated. Or we can plot the data as we do on the left side of the exhibit, where we show predicted versus actual values without a timeline. The closer these points appear to fit on a sloping line, the better the correlation. These charts could be comparing Google searches on "coupons" to inflation, tweets about the stock market to the Dow Jones, or Facebook connections to depression. It could be anything, but let's keep it generic for a moment.

Clearly, the chart on the top is a better fit than the one in the middle, which is better than the one on the bottom. The unaided eye can tell which model is doing well and which is doing poorly. The correlation, which is also represented by the symbol "R," is 0.9 in the top chart, 0.7 in the middle chart, and zero on the bottom. (If you want to see how these correlations are computed, you can see a spreadsheet on the book's Web site at www.pulsethenewscience.com.)

Note that a good or even an excellent fit does not mean a *perfect* fit. On any of these charts, you can find an "outlier," or an exception. Even so, it should be visually obvious now why the mere existence of outliers or the lack of a perfect correlation does not mean the same thing as no correlation at all. An imperfect correlation does not mean the model is useless.

There is a chance, however, that two random, independent variables could have a correlation as good or better than what is observed. This chance is referred to as the "p-value." A p-value of .25 means that there was a 25% chance that the two uncorrelated phenomena could appear to have a correlation. If the correlation R is not high and there are only a few data points, the p-value may show it might just be a fluke. If the correlation is very high or there are a large number of data points, then it would be extremely unlikely for an observed correlation to be a fluke. In most of the research I'll be reviewing, the latter is the case. The results are either highly correlated, based on a large number of data points, or both. In the research I will show, the math will show that it is almost impossible that such observations could be the result of chance. This is a critical point to make about the interpretation of statistical data, but it is a bit nuanced and it is lost on many people—especially in the media.

One example from the media shows two common misconceptions in use. In October 2010, two journalists on a CNBC news segment called "Squawk on the Street" were interviewing Johan Bollen, a researcher in the field of finding predictive utility in web activities. Bollen (who is discussed further in Chapter 7) had published convincing data that tweets predict moves in the Dow Jones. First, the journalists wondered how mundane tweets like "I'm going to the bathroom" could possibly be indicative of market moves.

To this, Bollen responded: "It's not so much the individual tweet that we are interested in, but sort of the pattern over millions of tweets being submitted on a daily basis. So it all adds up and provides us with some kind of a sense of what's going on." Bollen was correct. Contrary to the interviewer's intuition, the individual anecdote does not overturn the aggregate data. This fallacy is a recurring challenge whenever I present material like this to audiences. Someone will say, "Yes, but sometimes people tweet (or Google) for reasons unrelated to your measurement." The implication is that the mere existence of such "noise" in the data must therefore mean a complete lack of signal—even when the data is based on millions of samples. Obviously, variation in data exists in all the sciences, and this variation alone does not invalidate scientific inquiry. That is why a scientist takes a large number of samples. A single outlier in an R = 0.7 chart does not make the chart indistinguishable from an R = 0 chart.

The second interviewer noted that since Twitter users are younger and don't know much about investing, he "would question . . . whether they can be an indicator." This is the classic error of judging the data by a hypothesis instead of the other way around. Bollen's data showed that, in fact, there *was* a correlation between Tweets and moves in the market a couple of days later. The interviewer simply proposed a hypothesis that there *should* be no correlation because of the skewed demographic of Twitter users. Yet there *was* a correlation. Therefore, the interviewer's hypothesis that this source of noise would overwhelm the signal in the data is proven false by the Bollen's findings. If the interviewer had declared that the chart R = 0.9 above has an error that skews the results, then, clearly, this error could not be skewing the results very much.

If Bollen had proposed that he was going to start using Twitter to predict market moves without validating it against actual data of market moves, the interviewer's concern about this possible problem would certainly be valid. It would be unwise to have any confidence in such a claim until the data supported it. However, once the data shows the correlation, the hypothesis about how much noise is in the data has been addressed. As we shall see later, even seasoned researchers who reviewed some of the early research in this field made what amount to untested assumptions about the validity of data.

Another variation on the first misconception (the anecdotal error) is that if there are any other factors involved, then the observation that one factor correlates to an outcome is completely invalidated. When I tell audiences that searches on some words have a curiously strong correlation to future changes in the economy, at least one individual will point out that there are many possible causes for those changes. A person could search terms like "jobs" and "unemployment benefits" for a school paper or because of a news story about those topics. This is true—but it just means the correlation will not be perfect. The existence of other factors does not mean that there is no correlation at all. Look again at the middle charts with an R of 0.7. Clearly there are other factors that are not considered by the model; otherwise, it would be a better fit. But it is also very clear that this model does correlate at least somewhat with the observed value, and it is not indistinguishable from the R = 0 chart. In most cases, even a modest correlation like that is a big improvement on unaided human intuition when it comes to estimating or forecasting.

If objections like these were serious constraints to science, then very little science would ever get done. For example, my clients in the pharmaceutical industry certainly understand that there may be many factors in the healing of ulcers. But if hundreds of patients in a test group in a big drug trial recover from ulcers faster than the hundreds of patients in a control group taking a placebo, clearly the drug is working. Of course, there are probably factors that the medical profession does not even yet know of. Still, if the test group is healing faster than the control group at a statistically significant rate, then the drug is at least one factor. Again, the existence of noise is not the same as the lack of signal.

The last misconception worth mentioning is perhaps the most trivial of all, and I mention it only because I heard it more than a couple of times when discussing this topic. When researchers point out that search patterns, tweets, or purchases on eBay are correlated to some real-world phenomenon, some object based on the *one thing* they remember from first-semester statistics. "Aha, but correlation does not mean causation!" they shout. Yet nobody said it did. Correlation simply indicates that knowing one quantity reduces uncertainty about another quantity. If they would have remembered a bit *more* about their stats course, they would have recognized this.

If I had written an orbital mechanics simulator in Excel (which I have), I would be able to predict the position of a comet at a future date with some degree of accuracy. Obviously, my spreadsheet doesn't *cause* the asteroid to take the path it does. It just predicts it better than unaided intuition, and therein lays the utility. Correlations are useful because if I know one thing, then I am better at estimating another. And the same is true of the research I show starting in Chapter 5.

My first book, *How to Measure Anything*, was largely about addressing common fallacies regarding measurement and scientific method. Over and over again, half-remembered concepts about the rigor of science have convinced otherwise educated professionals that unless scientific research has perfect certainty, we actually learned nothing. In their minds, an imprecise number is no better than no number at all. This is, in fact, not the way scientific measurement really works. In my first book, I defined measurement in a way that is the closest to the de facto scientific use of the word: Measurement is the quantitative expression of a reduction of uncertainty from an observation (or set of observations).

As the mathematician Bertrand Russell put it, "Although this may seem a paradox, all exact science is based on the idea of approximation. If a man tells you he knows a thing exactly, then you can be safe in inferring that you are speaking to an inexact man." Many of the perceived problems with the research I'll be discussing are little more than misunderstandings about the meaning of measurement in science. Nowhere in science is measurement meant to be infinitely exact. A measurement simply has to result in less uncertainty than we had prior to the measurement. This is not only the scientific use of the word "measurement,"—it is the pragmatic use for business and government. If perfect certainty were required before every decision, management would always be in a state of perpetual inaction. We make measurements to make better bets. The Pulse will make many bets much, much better.

I sometimes see a printout of a quote in some information technology or engineering clients' project rooms that says: "Faster, Better, Cheaper—pick any two" (or "Fast, Good, Cheap—pick any two"). The Pulse actually is a far faster and cheaper predictor of economic activity and public opinion than traditional methods in many respects and it is also often a better one. With the Pulse, we can have all three. Next, Chapter 4 describes the structure of the Pulse that makes faster, better and cheaper possible. Chapters 5 through 10 prove "faster, better, and cheaper" is the case.

Notes

1. Measuring the Information Society—The ICT Development Index, International Telecommunications Union, 2009.
2. R. Sherman et al. "The Internet Gender Gap: Is It Narrowing or Widening?" Paper presented at the 107th Annual Convention of the American Psychiatric Association, Boston, August 1999.
3. A. Goldfarb and J. Prince. "Internet Adoption and Usage Patterns Are Different: Implications for the Digital Divide," *Information Economics and Policy* 20, no. 1 (March 2008): 2–15.
4. R. Vanniant and S. Lee. "Economic Characteristics of Internet Users vs. Nonusers and Implications of Web-Based Surveys," *Webuse@Society* 1, no. 8 (Winter 2005): 34–51.
5. D. Graham-Rowe and W. Knight. "Internet Users More Chic than Geek," *New Scientist*, November 26, 2001; www.newscientist.com/article/dn1606-internet-users-more-chic-than-geek.html.
6. Alexa has verified that this is not merely bad data. Policy changes at Google—which has owned Youtube since 2006—are the likely explanation. In 2009 Google ceased to allow users to upload videos to Google video. This may have begun to push more traffic to Youtube. Then, suddenly, at the beginning of 2010, some significant portion of traffic going to Youtube was sent back to Google. I could not determine the exact cause of this.
7. W. Wee. November 16, 2010, "MySpace's New Strategy: It's No Longer a Social Network."

CHAPTER 4

Dynamics of the Pulse

As in geology, so in social institutions, we may discover the causes of all past changes in the present invariable order of society.

—Henry David Thoreau

Online activities will change over time, and certainly individual online service providers will change. But what will be more persistent is the fundamental structure of incentives and technology that will continue to make so much of our online activity publicly available for the Pulse. None of the activities on the Internet would be useful for tracking macrotrends if both users and providers of online services had no incentive to share data. Users need some reason to provide their own data for public consumption, and online services need some reason to make that data public, even if only in some highly aggregated form devoid of individual private information. Otherwise, the data generated by our online purchases, game playing, searching, and so on would stay sequestered in confidential databases of such services as Amazon, eBay, Google, and Twitter.

But, fortunately for the Pulse, there are many reasons why users and online service providers do share this data and will continue to do so. Let's briefly talk about the incentives, some of the technologies, the distribution of the Internet, and how these all interact in a system that produces a Pulse and that will endure changes in players and technology.

Incentives: Why the Pulse Exists

The Internet and the Pulse are not one in the same. The Pulse is a subset of the Internet that consists only of publicly available information. But, like the Internet, the Pulse probably is here to stay for reasons that go beyond current technologies or social fads. Users are incentivized to volunteer information, and service providers in turn are incentivized to share that information to a wider public. The various technical methods of collecting this information make it all possible, but the fundamental incentives will ensure that the Pulse persists and grows.

The data of the Pulse starts with end users of some service on the Internet. Users provide data either for its own end or because they have to reveal it to get other things they want.

1. *Posting for the purpose of posting.* In some cases, the data is shared because that is the fundamental point of the service and the reason you visit the site. Twitter and Facebook are entirely about the user-generated content that other users can see. Users generate video blogs on YouTube or create product reviews on Amazon because they expect the service provider to make it publicly available. The posting could be anonymous or with the user's real name, but as long as the posting is public, it is part of the Pulse. In this case, the user and the online service provider have the same objective.

2. *Posting as a means to an end.* In other cases, users' objectives are not necessarily to post their data for the world to see, but they still provide data either actively or passively. In order to make purchases from services like Amazon or eBay, for example, we need to know things like price and availability. Unlike blogging, posting this data is not its own reward. On eBay, users have to provide information, such as the price they are willing to pay—just to participate in an auction. Likewise, simply visiting a site or watching a YouTube video updates information, such as the traffic to the site or the total viewer count of a video. In some cases, users may not even be aware they are providing data, but their activities leave a data trail, nonetheless, even if it is in some highly aggregated form.

Service providers, in turn, offer this data and make it available to others besides the users who provided the data. The reasons a service provider does this can be grouped into three general categories. The incentive to do so may be to facilitate other activities, to simply to draw people to a site, and, in some cases, it appears that providers offer the data simply because they can.

1. The information may have to be provided because the site cannot do what it does if it doesn't provide it. When you bid on auctions on eBay, you, of course, have to see the previous bids or whether the item was already sold. This isn't just part of the site's draw. It is a necessary part of bidding, which is the central point of the site. Perhaps the information itself is part of what users are paying for, like the search data offered to Google Adword buyers.

2. The online service provider may provide this information because it is part of the draw of the site and other users find some value in it; this is the case with the Amazon book sales ranks. Amazon displays the "sales rank" of a book indicating that a book ranks, for example, 527th or 19,245th in sales compared to all other books on Amazon. Displaying this information has little to do with the function of the site; you didn't make your book purchase in order to make a minute change to the book's sales rank. But other Amazon users find it at least entertaining—and perhaps even useful in the purchase decision—to know how popular a book is. Like data about the number of viewers of a Youtube video, Amazon book ranks are highly aggregated and say nothing about individual purchases.

3. In rarer, but prominent, cases, online services offer information to the public without knowing what it will be for and simply because they can. For example, Google set up Google Trends to make search volumes on some keywords publicly available without knowing how much interest it would generate. Twitter is providing—for free—access to some or all of its tweets without any good plan as to how this will generate revenue for the site. (At the time of the writing of this book, Twitter has not managed to generate revenue.) Twitter offers the data because it can and it wants to see what will happen. Amazon book sales may fall in this category since I don't know for a fact that Amazon knew that the rankings might be a draw when it started posting them.

The Systems behind Getting and Sharing Data

The Pulse would not be very useful if we had to surf thousands of sites and manually track data. The information is made accessible by being gathered and distributed in some automated way. In the next list, the first four examples are methods that facilitate the gathering of information. The last two items address how that data might be captured and how other parties might be involved. In all cases, the original source of the data was the same—millions of end users every day were navigating the web, entering data, and clicking on buttons to build this massive data set.

1. *Direct downloads.* Some service providers make it very easy to get a Pulse without any technical background at all. The Web site may allow you to download data directly to a spreadsheet or some other common format. Google Trends and Google Adwords both do this. This topic was reviewed briefly in Chapter 1, but we will get further into it in Chapter 5.

2. *Screen scraper.* Also called "HTML[1] scrapers," these programs will grab anything you are able to see on any Web site and store it in your own files. For example, I might want to track all the sales ranks of books on Amazon that are related to foreclosures. Or I might want to track how often late-model cars are sold on eBay and at what price. (These kinds of data might be useful in tracking economic trends.) Screen scraper software goes to each page you tell it to visit—even if it is thousands of pages—and grabs what you need directly off the page. Even Excel has a simple version of this you can try. In Office 2007 or later, there is an option under "Data" in the "Get External Data" box. There you can choose "From Web." A navigation window will open, and you can select data from the Web. Each time the screen is refreshed, Excel checks that data again. There are also screen scrapers you can download for free trial periods, such as www.screen-scraper.com.

3. *Application Program Interface (API).* The API is a tool that gives developers direct access to the same data you could have gotten with a screen scraper. APIs are usually provided by the online services themselves but sometimes they can be created by third parties. Some services sell their APIs, but many are available for free. Most of the major sites have one or more APIs with documentation for developers that can be downloaded from their sites. Service providers may set limits, such as a number of queries per day an API can make. Like the direct download method, APIs are exclusively provided by the Web site service they access, and it is entirely up to the service whether they want to modify or even drop an API. See Exhibit 4.1 for a list of key APIs of the major sources of data discussed so far.

4. *Crawlers.* A crawler is a program that systematically visits a large number of Web sites and records something about them. Unlike APIs, which typically are provided by service providers of individual Web sites, crawlers are developed by other parties, similar to HTML scrapers. While crawlers do "scrape" data similar to HTML scrapers, crawlers visit many more sites with an expanding search pattern. As a crawler visits a site, it records links to other sites and puts them in the queue for further crawling. Crawlers are primarily used by search engines to index the World Wide Web, but they do have other applications. Archival applications such as the Wayback Machine record versions of Web sites for future references. In principle, crawlers can be used to gather data for the Pulse.

5. *Tools for users.* Some online services may offer a toolbar, app (application), or plug-in that provides functionality to users specifically in exchange for the ability to access data about those users. By themselves, these tools are not part of the Pulse because they are usually used to generate data for the use of a single organization. I mention this

Web Site	API Name	Data Downloaded
Google	pyGTrends*	A CSV file containing Google Trends data for a set of keywords
	Social Graph API	Web addresses of public pages, and publicly declared connections between them
Facebook	Graph API	Users, Facebook applications, pages, groups, photos, photo albums, geolocations, comments, events, friends lists, status messages and wall posts**
Twitter	Twitter API	Public timelines, friends' timelines, followers, friends, locations for which trending topics exist, trending topics for a location, current top trending topics, daily top trending topics, and weekly top trending topics
eBay	Finding API	Recommended keywords for a given search term, find items by keywords, by category, by a product identifier or by other "advanced" criteria
	Price Research API	Basic pricing statistics for a keyword and date range combination
	Advanced Research API*	Item information for a rolling 90-day history, including items by category, pricing statistics for a given keyword search, raw item data for a keyword search, information about the usage of the title suggestion tool, and user statistics
Amazon	Product Advertising API	New and used item information (Actor, Author, Brand, Publisher, Price, etc. . .), Seller information (feedback rating, legal name, ID, "glance page", etc. . .), items by seller lookup, and a huge amount of data pertaining to specific types of items

*Third-party API
**The app must get explicit permission from users even if the data is already publicly available.

EXHIBIT 4.1   Key Application Program Interfaces for Data Access

primarily because it is one of the ways that service providers or third parties can obtain information that they then may elect to make available to the public. Alexa.com (which also runs the Wayback Machine) gathers some of its information from a toolbar feature it offers. Mobile phone apps that make restaurant recommendations use your location when you search for recommended places that are nearby. Such mobile apps are a particularly important and growing area that is already the focus of some new research. Interesting examples of apps like these can be found on the book's Web site at www.pulsethenewscience.com.

6. *Third-party developers.* Third-party developers are not a technology in themselves, but part of the system in which the technology may be made available to others. Some developers have already taken APIs, end user tools, and HTML scrapers and crawlers to create Web sites that offer this information—sometimes for free and sometimes for a fee. The developers may use the APIs to generate data available on their own sites or they may use an API as part of an app they sell. I track the Amazon sales ranks of my books with www.metricjunkie.com. I have been investigating Metric Junkie as a possible leading indicator of other big trends. It uses the Amazon APIs to develop a site that can create a chart of how the ranks of books change over time. This is a free service offered to drive sales to the books being tracked. (Metric Junkie is part of the Amazon "affiliates program," so they get a small commission for each book sold to visitors of Metric Junkie's site.) Other developers, such as www.terapeak.com, have taken APIs from eBay to offer analysis of the site's auction history. Sites like this may come and go so check out www.pulsethenewscience.com for a current listing.

Collaboration and Competition

The combination of technologies and the incentives for users and service providers generate a dynamic system of collaboration and competition based on both carrots and sticks. The API and scraper balance is one example of this. Online services don't generally want people to get their data with scrapers because scrapers slow down their network. If there is a demand for data, the threat of screen scrapers is a strong motivation for online services to give out APIs.

Mark Barros of Metric Junkie says, "Sometimes APIs are too narrow and people go back to HTML scrapers, which defeats the point of the API." Barros recalled one specific situation where a service provider created a backlash. "In the fall of 2009, Amazon APIs stopped providing access to Kindle data because Amazon decided not to pay commissions under the affiliate program. So some developers just went back to scraping."

Or you could use crawlers to gather the data you need from as many sites as you like. The Robot Exclusion Protocol tries to frame a kind of agreement about who can crawl what. Sites can post a file called "robots.txt" on their site; the file tells crawlers whether they are welcome. Unfortunately for site owners, crawlers can simply ignore this file and get the data anyway. Web developers and site administrators put a lot of value on "playing nice" without much of a threat of legal or other punitive action other than simply being ostracized by the web community.

Service providers and third-party providers are another dynamic balance on the Pulse. Online service providers generally are interested in the creation of third-party data aggregation sources and apps. These sites or tools increase the value of the service providers' own service to customers, and some online providers encourage the development of the third-party providers. Third parties that build businesses on the availability of this data are displaying a lot of trust. A business like Terapeak, for example, could be at risk if eBay changes in some fundamental way or disables its APIs.

Analysts seeking to measure the Pulse on some topic could always resort to scraping if the online service ceases to provide APIs or direct downloads. But usually there is little analysts can do if the service decides not to disclose the data on its screen. If, for example, Amazon decides not to show the sales ranking of a book, or if Google decides not to provide search volumes on a given term, then there is little the information seeker could do to change it.

However, there is no incentive for Google, Amazon, Yahoo!, eBay, or others to capriciously terminate a public information source once it has been available for a period of time. The network of third-party services that depend on APIs or information otherwise available through scraping add value to the service. Metric Junkie drives some sales to Amazon by showing historical book sales rank data. Terapeak, no doubt, makes eBay more useful to many sellers.

There is some volatility among major online services. As previously mentioned, Myspace quickly lost all its dominance in social media to Facebook, and at one time Yahoo! was the dominant search engine over Google. But the basic structure of these technologies and incentives probably will make the Pulse available indefinitely.

Power Law: Why a Few Sources Tell Us a Lot on the Internet

A general law of nature has to do with how big and small things are distributed, and this law has two parts:

1. There are relatively few big things and lots of small things.
2. However, a few big things are bigger than most of the little things combined.

The Internet follows a law like this. This means that most of the data we need for the Pulse tends to be concentrated in a few major sources. This fact is particularly useful for the Pulse. Laws that describe the distribution of big things and small things often fall under a broad category of models called "power laws."

You might see one version of this rule called the *Pareto Law*. There are rules of thumb about this expressed in business as the 80/20 rule, 90/10 rule, or something similar (e.g., perhaps 20% of a business's inventory generates 80% of its revenue or 10% of its customers generate 90% of customer support costs). These distributions of large and small things tend to fit a particular mathematical model surprisingly often. Various versions of these mathematical rules are all part of a larger set of observed rules, the power laws. We will look at one particular version called *Zipf's law*.

Zipf's law is based on a statistical observation made in 1935 by a linguist named George Kinsley Zipf. Zipf showed that the distribution of word frequencies in languages followed a consistent pattern. The second most frequently used word was used about half as often as the first, the third most used word was used about a third as often, and so on. There are exceptions, of course, but over thousands of words, this rule was a pretty good fit. Other researchers generalized this law and showed that the pattern applied to many other phenomena, such as the size of asteroids, the incomes of individuals, the population of cities, and the sizes of earthquakes and plagues. Zipf's law can be expressed as

$$y = 1/x^a$$

where

$y =$ some quantity that will be rank-ordered (e.g., word frequency, size of an earthquake, duration of a power outage, etc.)

$x =$ rank of a value in a list of values

$a =$ a constant very close to 1

For example, if we are using Zipf's law to describe the distribution of human heights, x would be your rank by height among a group of people (say, you are the 342nd tallest person in your firm) and y is your actual height.

Suppose we rank all of the Web sites in the world by the amount of traffic that they get so that rank 1 would be the site with the highest traffic, 2 with the second highest, and so forth. Then, suppose we plot the ranks and the actual daily traffic on a chart. Of course, by definition, we would expect to see that as the rank gets higher, the traffic gets lower (e.g., the traffic to the 63rd most visited site has less traffic than the 62nd most visited site). What is interesting is that this decrease in traffic as a function of traffic rank follows a very specific pattern. This pattern becomes visible if we plot these values on a log/log chart, where each value is shown as its logarithm and each increment higher is actually a factor of 10 times greater. Exhibit 4.2 shows this data from Alexa.com.

We see that as the ranks go from 1, to 10, to 100, and so on, the worldwide share of traffic decreases at a fairly predictable rate. The data

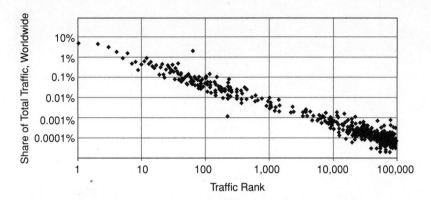

EXHIBIT 4.2 Distribution of Sites by Traffic Rank and Share of Total Traffic

does not fit a perfect line only because rank changed faster than the data could be gathered. Still, it is clear that as the rank number increases by a factor of 10, the traffic volume decreases by about a factor of 10. Conveniently, this rule applies to other aspects of the Internet. If Web site traffic, search engine use, online auctions, or friend networks were more evenly distributed, we might have to look at a much larger subset of the Internet to get a representative Pulse.

As another example, take the distribution of time spent on sites as shown in Exhibit 4.3. I'm showing the site rank as a surrogate for "time

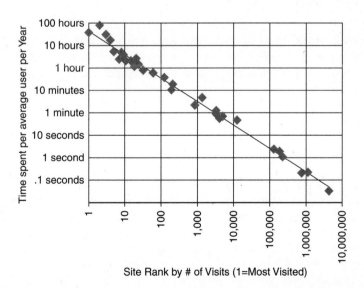

EXHIBIT 4.3 Distribution of Time Spent per Site per User on Average Worldwide

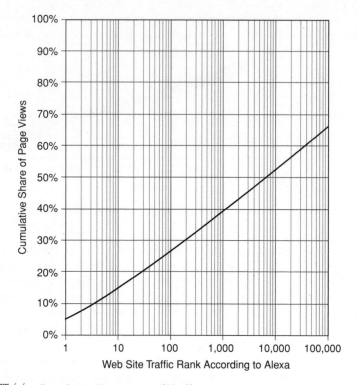

EXHIBIT 4.4   Cumulative Percentage of Traffic

spent rank," since Alexa doesn't explicitly provide that rank—so, again, the data does not fit a perfect line. Even so, the data still shows a strong Zipf's law pattern. This distribution pattern facilitates data analysis by getting a high bang for the buck by looking at the top-ranked data sources. Where people spend the most time is generally also where they enter a lot of data.

If we can compare either of these data sets to the total size of the web, we find that the top few sources give us a disproportionately large share of the web's total traffic and user-time spent. Exhibit 4.4 shows us how the top sites account for most of the traffic. Estimates vary on the size of the web, but it is safe to say that there are hundreds of millions of Web sites. Yet, this Zipf's law pattern shows us that the top sites make up a big part of that traffic. The top 10 sites alone make up 15% of all traffic—as much as the next 1,000 sites combined. And the top 100 make up as much traffic as the next 10,000 combined. And the top 10,000 take up half of all traffic, leaving the other 300 million or so sites to divide up the rest.

This distribution pattern also appears to be a fairly stable characteristic of the Internet. As far back as 1997, a study of America Online users showed that a very similar Zipf's law applied to the number of unique visitors per day and links to sites.[2] Still, while the overall distribution may be constant, individual players may change quickly. Sites shoot up and down this ranking, and that is why we need fairly regular monitoring of where most people actually are putting their daily digital record of Internet activities.

So far, I have introduced the basic idea of the Pulse, explained how it is different from traditional methods of measuring the world, and described some of the systems and incentives that make it possible. Next we look at recent research that shows scientific evidence that we can track and predict macro-trends in economics, health, and society as a whole by using the Pulse.

Notes

1. HyperText Markup Language
2. L. Adamic and H. Bernardo. "Zipf's Law and the Internet." *Glattometrics 3*. 2002. 143–150.

PART II

Sources of the Pulse

CHAPTER 5

What Our Surfing Says

Harnessing the collective intelligence of millions of users, Google web search logs can provide one of the most timely, broad reaching influenza monitoring systems available today.

—February 2009 article in *Nature*[1]

The Internet contains an enormous amount of information which, to our knowledge, classical econometrics has yet to appropriately tap into.

—2009 article in *Applied Economics Quarterly*[2]

Depending on the source we use to track search engine use, Internet users in the United States average about 30 minutes to an hour each week using search tools like Google, Bing, or Yahoo!—although mostly Google at the time this book was written. Google takes over 66% of all online queries totaling about half a billion searches a day on topics ranging from child care, politics, vacation spots, home buying, to jobs.[3]

Any decision we think we are about to make is something that can be Googled before we commit to a choice. As a result, Internet searches become a way to signal not just what we are doing but what we intend to do. For more and more of us, searching the Internet is the *first* thing we do when we have a car problem, a tax question, an upcoming major purchase, a legal problem, or even just the sniffles.

Google, like its competitors, gets almost all of its revenue from advertising. Google generates over $21 billion per year from selling what it calls "Adwords," using a kind of dynamic auction process. People who want their product or service to occupy one of the coveted top-of-page positions when someone uses Google bid on how much they are willing to pay per click. The advertiser may bid a few cents or a few dollars but is charged only if a user clicks on the advertiser's link. To determine how close a given advertiser gets to the top of the page, Google applies an algorithm that considers the bid as well as the relevance and quality factors of a potential search result.

The reason this keyword bidding process is important for the Pulse is because of the additional information search engines provide their advertisers. For example, Google provides detailed information about how often the search terms you bid on are used and the general geographic location of the person doing the search. Advertisers then can use information about the effectiveness of their search terms to modify the Adwords they bid on.

But since 2006, you don't even have to be a Google advertiser to see this data. Google decided to present a version of this information in "Google Trends" and then in the slightly more advanced "Google Insights for Search" services. These services tell anyone who is interested the relative frequency of use of a particular search term from as far back as January 1, 2004, and up to yesterday. As long as the search term meets some minimum volume, Google will present the data.

Using the frequency of use of search terms as a research tool is recent and still controversial. Skeptics questioned the validity of this kind of research, but eventually even prestigious academic journals were willing to publish research in this area. This chapter looks at how research in using Google searches as macroscopic measures of society first evolved from a new way to detect possible influenza outbreaks. We look at a simple example you can try yourself, and we show how this method has been applied to major purchasing decisions for real estate, cars, and electronics.

Tracking Flu Outbreaks: A Faster, Better, and Cheaper Method

One of the first inklings of using the Internet's Pulse in a practical way came from an epidemiologist at the University of Toronto named Gunther Eysenbach. In the days when Google was still just a research project conducted by two Stanford PhD candidates, Eyesenbach was interested in how health information is disseminated. This interest evolved soon after finishing medical school in Munich and Freiberg, Germany, when in 1996 Eysenbach helped create a Web site on dermatology. At the time, the assumed purpose of this site was to provide a place for information exchange among medical colleagues. Then Eysenbach found that most of the visits were not from doctors but from patients.

Health information was already becoming readily available on the Internet, and Eysenbach thought this might be an interesting new field of research. According to Pew Research, about three-quarters of all adults who are online have used the Internet to search for health-related information. But this easy availability of health information also had a downside: A lot of it was wrong. Eysenbach found that misinformation about health issues spread by word of mouth and by the Internet similar to how a virus would spread.

He coined the term *infodemiology* to mean the epidemiology of how health information spreads. Eysenbach began to realize early in his new research that in the course of seeking information about health (whether the information was accurate or not), people were also saying something about their health or the health of someone close to them. By 2004, he devised a way to use Google's Adword service to get information on the spikes in searches like "flu symptoms" or "treating a flu" and the cities where those spikes occurred. He would then compare this to the traditional information-gathering system used in Canada.

The conventional influenza reporting process is based on the "sentinel" system. Sentinel doctors and hospitals have a direct line of communication to a public health authority, such as the Centers for Disease Control and Prevention (CDC) in the United States or the Centre for Infectious Disease Prevention and Control in Canada. Similar systems exist throughout the developed world and are the basis of all infectious disease monitoring. This reporting method is known to have a lag of one to two weeks—a significant period of time that could make the difference in timeliness of intervention decisions. Health authorities, if they knew about a flu outbreak soon enough, could minimize the impact by executing a media campaign for public health warnings, implementing additional safety procedures at hospitals, or even using more drastic interventions, such as travel restrictions or canceling public events. Given the emergence of strains like H1N1 and H1N5, this delay could be the difference between a temporary inconvenience for the public and a tragic health crisis.

Prior to Eysenbach's study, researchers knew that other behaviors might be indicators of flu outbreaks. Calls to flu information centers and the sales of certain over-the-counter medicines had already been found to have strong correlations to actual reported outbreaks. Given the frequent use of the Internet as a health information source, Eyesenbach's study seemed like the logical next step.

Eysenbach began using his new method using Google Adwords during the 2004–2005 flu season. During this period, Eysenbach received 54,507 "impressions" from Google, indicating the total number of times his ad was shown, whether the user clicked on it or not. Of those, 4,582 generated a "click-through" for Eysenbach. Since he bid a maximum of 8 cents for each click-through (the actual cost of a click could be less, depending on the other bidders) the total cost of the Adwords came to a total of $365.64 for the entire flu season.

Yet this was far from a you-get-what-you-pay-for situation. Eysenbach's inexpensive flu tracking method actually predicted the flu cases

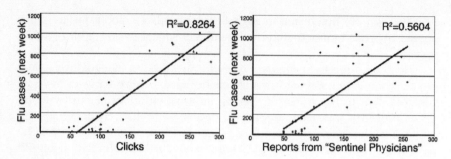

EXHIBIT 5.1   Clicks versus Clinical: Original Charts from Dr. Gunther Eysenbach's Study

Source: Gunther Eysenbach

of the following week *better than the reports of the sentinel physicians.* Exhibit 5.1 shows the original charts from Eysenbach's published study. In these he shows a common measure of how well two data sets "fit," R^2. This is simply the square of the correlation R mentioned in Chapter 3. The R^2 can be interpreted as the amount of variance in one variable that is explained by the other variable. (For a spreadsheet example of this calculation, go to www.pulsethenewscience.com.)

When comparing the reports of sentinel physicians to the flu cases of the next week, Eysenbach computed an R^2 of 0.5604. For clicks versus flu cases of the next week, he got an R^2 of 0.8264. To a statistician, this is a big difference. But you can see the difference just with your eyes. If you tried to predict next week's flu cases using the traditional method, you would have much more error than if you simply predicted it based on the number of clicks.

Eysenbach told me he sent his paper to 10 journals, all of which turned him down. "A lot of reviewers said it was interesting but correlations with Internet behavior don't tell us anything," Eysenbach recalled. Eventually, he was able to get it published in the American Medical Informatics Association (AMIA) 2006 symposium proceedings.[4] (The AMIA actually caters more to information systems professionals working in the healthcare industry, not to epidemiologists.) To the reviewers for the journals that rejected Eysenbach's research, activity on the Internet was entirely the opposite of "proper" research in epidemiology. Epidemiology, in their minds, was structured and based on serious data collected by serious people. What people did on the Internet was unstructured and unserious. It was even downright silly much of the time. How can Internet buzz be the least bit enlightening about the very serious topic of disease outbreaks?

This is an example of one of the classic errors of the interpretation of statistics mentioned in Chapter 3, and it is one that even many scientific professionals make about the interpretation of data. They have made a hypothesis about what they believe *ought* to happen with the data and ignore what *did* happen. Understandably, scientists need to test claims based on overwhelming evidence. The evidence is considered "statistically valid" if it is highly improbable that the observations could be due to chance rather than saying anything about the truth of the claim being tested. This rigor is central to scientific method. However, even as scientists, they hold one assumption to be true without any such evidence: They assume that the underlying data itself is spurious and unreliable even when the results themselves contradict that assumption.

However, as mentioned in Chapter 3, this statement about the data is merely an assumption, and even this assumption is a testable claim. The strong correlations alone should have been enough to cause Eysenbach's reviewers to doubt the assumptions they were making about his data set. Their assumptions about data noise are not a standard by which real empirical evidence in judged. On the contrary, empirical data is the standard by which their assumptions should be judged.

Eventually the resistance to this new way of tracking and predicting flu outbreaks would wane. A study by another group of researchers using Yahoo! to predict flu outbreaks was published in 2008 and also showed promising results. This time, the study covered four flu seasons of data and was published in a journal much more relevant to epidemiology, *Clinical Infectious Diseases*.[5] This study did not directly compare clicks to physicians' reports, but it did show that searches correlated to actual flu outbreaks. Although this study showed more modest R^2 results than Eysenbach's study, its much larger data set could show that the relationship between searches and flu outbreaks is almost certainly a real phenomenon.

But Eysenbach would be vindicated again by an even more prestigious publication. By February 2009, Lynnette Brammer from Google along with five researchers from the CDC brought the topic of the correlations between Internet searches and flu outbreaks to a new level of scientific respectability by getting the idea published in the scientific journal *Nature*,[6] one of the most prestigious science journals that any scientist could ever hope to be published in.

Nature focuses on what the editors consider to be groundbreaking discoveries in a field. World-changing ideas—the structure of DNA, plate tectonics, the discovery of nuclear fission, and animal cloning—were all reported for the first time on the pages of this journal. Because articles are required to be groundbreaking, editors reject the majority of submitted articles even before subjecting them to peer review. It is fairly likely that at least some of the reviewers who originally rejected Eysenbach's article proposal have long sought, unsuccessfully, to be published in *Nature*. They must be kicking themselves, now.

It is worth noting at this point that despite multiple previous studies (more listed later in this chapter) confirming a correlation between search behavior and flu outbreaks, a 2010 study conducted by the CDC found that the tool Google Flu Trends (which emerged in 2008, after Eysenbach's work) did *not* predict actual influenza quite as well as lab-confirmed, positive results for influenza.[7] Of course, you would have to *wait* for the lab results, but they are the ultimate standard of whether actual influenza exists. (The flu virus does not always cause a flu-like illness.) This study showed that Google was 25% less accurate in predicting actual influenza, but that it is accurate in predicting "influenza-like" illness. Obviously, when people first search on this topic, they apparently only suspect they have a flu, they haven't confirmed it.

The CDC study simply provided a useful caution about interpreting the data. At no point does the CDC study deny a clear correlation between search behaviors and actual influenza as well as influenza-like illness. When the findings are compared carefully, the CDC study doesn't directly contradict any of the findings published in *Nature* nor those published by Eysenbach or other researchers. The CDC study does not contradict Eysenbach's finding that search behavior is better than sentinel physicians (who don't always have lab tests before they make a diagnosis) and, in fact, confirms that there is a strong correlation—though obviously not a perfect one—between searches and influenza.

Even though the CDC findings only showed that the Google method was a little less accurate (although much faster) in predicting lab-confirmed influenza, the headlines in the press were "Google Flu Trends Do Not Match CDC Data."[8] Two data sets hardly ever "match" perfectly if they come from real-world measurements. But headlines like this would imply, to average news readers who don't understand the value of correlations, that the flu trends data was useless. In effect, they might conclude that if R^2 is not equal to 1, then it is no better than 0.

This uphill climb for Eysenbach is an example of history repeating itself. Dr. John Snow's challenges a century and a half ago show that, in some ways, thinking has not changed much. Recall that Snow tried to show that cholera was waterborne instead of airborne; even convincing evidence was not enough at first. Since the health authorities were convinced that cholera was an airborne disease (an idea based on nothing like the evidence Snow had compiled), their assumption was that Snow's evidence must be in error, not their airborne hypothesis. Entrenched ideas are hard to overcome even when trained scientists are confronted with overwhelming evidence and the issue is something as critical as public health.

A Do-It-Yourself Pulse Tracking Example: Using Google Trends for Economic Predictions

In November 2005, while Gunther Eysenbach was gathering data and trying to get his manuscript accepted for publication, three business school professors managed to publish a promising study about predicting economic trends with search data.[9] Michael Ettredge and Gilbert Karunga from the University of Kansas along with John Gerdes from the University of California–Riverside published their research in a journal about computing, not econometrics, and it was a very small study with a small data set.

They found small but statistically significant correlations between official unemployment statistics and a fairly elaborate model that aggregated several searches related to unemployment. The article does not disclose the specific model, but it could have used search terms like "jobs," "work," or "unemployment benefits." Although the authors indicated much interest in additional research on the topic, it does not appear that they continued to investigate it as the adoption of the Internet increased and search tools improved. If they had had a much more powerful tool, like Google Trends, they might have been able to develop a more powerful predictive model. Now, we will use that tool to do what those earlier researchers probably wish they could have done.

Google Trends is perhaps the simplest publicly available method for tracking the Pulse on a topic. The data is immediately accessible to anyone and can be exported in a useful spreadsheet form without any technical knowledge. In Chapter 1, we briefly discussed a simple example where we looked up Google Trends data for "coupons." Now we go a bit deeper into the interpretation, uses, and limits of that kind of information by looking at the search frequency on the term "unemployment." This will also give us an opportunity to compare the Pulse to a major measurement effort using traditional survey methods—the national unemployment rate as computed by Bureau of Labor Statistics (BLS).

Searches on a term like "unemployment" could tell us something about actual unemployment. People who are unemployed may search for "unemployment benefits" or seek the location of the "unemployment office." Obviously, there are many reasons why biases in Google searches might mean that search volumes are not a reflection of real trends like unemployment. We know that people who use the Internet are not a uniform cross-section of society. People with low incomes or little education are much less likely to use the Internet and, for that matter, Google. We also know that people who search on the term "unemployment" may simply be seeking more information about national unemployment rates recently reported in news media.

However, as I pointed out before, whether the alleged biases *actually do* wipe out any correlation in the data is a testable hypothesis. In the case of unemployment, we have access to extensive data from the BLS, part of the U.S. Department of Commerce. The BLS report has a lag of three to five weeks on the period of time it is measuring; in contrast, the Google Trends data is available soon after midnight at the end of the week being measured. If the Google Trends on the word "unemployment" is a good predictor of the BLS data, then we know that any alleged bias is limited.

The BLS Current Population Survey (CPS), which is the basis of official unemployment figures, is a classic example of a massive survey methodology for tracking macro-trends. The reported unemployment rate is based on a random sample of 60,000 households conducted every month. (The unemployment rate report should not be confused with the *employment* report, which is based on employer surveys.) The survey does not collect data for the entire month but for only a single week called the "reference week"—the week that contains the 12th day of the month. The survey consists of several questions used to determine whether people are working and, if not, whether they are looking for work, able to work, and at least 16 years old. Retired millionaires or the infirm, for example, are not counted among the unemployed.

Each household is surveyed for four consecutive months. The first interview is conducted in person, and the other three are generally conducted by phone. Each month one-quarter of the 60,000 households are new and a quarter are rolled off the survey. Households are then given an eight-month break, then reenter the survey for another four-month period before they are permanently retired from the sample.

The survey is conducted by personnel from the Census Bureau who may also be allocated to other tasks at other times. For this reason, total figures regarding the number of staff members needed by the BLS and Census to gather and analyze data every month is hard to come by. But by simply estimating typical time required for 7,500 in-person interviews and the 52,500 phone interviews all to be conducted within a period of about two weeks after the reference week, we can be sure that it takes well over 100 people to conduct the interviews alone. More personnel would be needed for collection process management, data analysis, and information technology support. The total cost of computing the monthly unemployment rate is easily tens of millions of dollars per year.

Even with this extensive effort, economists say that this method may still underestimate unemployment as we might usually define the term. Using "actively seeking employment" as a criterion for being unemployed probably does omit some people who gave up looking. Some sources, such as the independent (non-government) Shadow Government Statistics (SGS) service, attempts to correct for this. But what is interesting is that the "real" unemployment rate that the SGS estimates, while being higher than the official unemployment rate, is higher by a fairly consistent amount. The "adjusted" and "official" unemployment trends are running virtually parallel, but the adjusted rate is about twice that of the official one. Because of its consistency, this type of error can be easily corrected, if necessary. And since one rate shadows the other so closely, if either is correlated to Google Trends, the other will be, too.

SGS attempts to correct for what is called a *systemic* error. A systemic error is a consistent bias and it is a function of how the survey is conducted, not the sample size. Random errors, however, usually are more of a function of the survey size and consistency of measurement. But the large size of the CPS sample and its highly consistent application means that random error in this study would be less than one fifth of 1%. Even with its faults, the BLS report is still based on the most extensive and thoroughly scrutinized source on the U.S. unemployment levels (using traditional methods). Now, let's see how this official source compares to the Pulse as measured with Google Trends.

As explained in Chapter 1, we go to www.google.com/trends and type in our search term of interest: unemployment. You will see a chart called the "Search Volume index" showing the relative volumes of searches on the term going back to January 1, 2004. Notice that from mid-2004 to about mid-2008, the level of searches on the word "unemployment" was fairly steady. Then, by the fall of 2008, the rate of searches on the word rose dramatically. By January 2009, the searches had doubled from the 2004 to 2008 rates.

You will also notice that another chart just below it called the "News reference volume." This chart indicates how often the term appeared in on-line news media sources. At first glance, you might think the increase in the search volume might be due to people simply responding to what they hear on the news about unemployment. But remember, the official unemployment numbers for a given reference week aren't released for another three to five weeks after Google releases its data and the news media depend almost entirely on the BLS report for data. If we find a correlation between the unemployment for a given period and the search volume, it can't simply be because people are reacting to the news; that news will not be out for about another month.

You will need to sign in with a Google account at the top right corner of the screen (or register for an account if you don't have one already) in order to go further. Once you have an account, you can start the following procedure:

1. Go to www.google.com/trends, sign in, type in "unemployment," and hit return. The chart showing the search volume of the term "unem-ployment" will appear.

	A	B	C	D
1	unemployment	unemployment	(std error)	
2	1	0%		
3				
4				
5	Week	unemployment	unemployment	(std error)
6	Jan 4 2004	1.1	2%	
7	Jan 11 2004	1.02	2%	
8	Jan 18 2004	1.02	2%	
9	Jan 25 2004	1.02	2%	
10	Feb 1 2004	1	2%	
11	Feb 8 2004	0.92	2%	
12	Feb 15 2004	0.9	2%	
13	Feb 22 2004	0.88	2%	
14	Feb 29 2004	0.98	3%	
15	Mar 7 2004	0.8	3%	
16	Mar 14 2004	0.88	2%	
17	Mar 21 2004	0.78	3%	
18	Mar 28 2004	0.96	2%	

Week ending the most recent Sunday

EXHIBIT 5.2   CSV File with Relative Scaling Exported from Google Trends

2. On the bottom left of the page (below the bar charts for regions and cities), you will see a + symbol and the phrase "Export this page as a CSV file." If you click on the + symbol, you will be given a choice of "CSV with relative scaling" and "CSV with fixed scaling." For now, pick the former. The CSV, or "comma separated value," file will open as an Excel spreadsheet. Exhibit 5.2 shows what this output looks like in a spreadsheet. The most recent week of data will be the week ending on the last Sunday. (If you have trouble with this step, try choosing "Save As" after clicking on relative scaling, save it as an Excel file, and open in Excel.)

3. Remove all but the "reference week" (the week that contains the 12th day of the month) rows of data from this table. (This is a little tedious, so feel free to skip to the example in this book's blog at www.pulsethenewscience.com.) When this is done, each month will have only one row of data. In addition, remove the "standard error" column so that only the actual unemployment rate remains for each month.

4. Now, we need to compare this to BLS data. Go to the BLS page at www.bls.gov/webapps/legacy/cpsatab1.htm.

5. You will see Table A-1. Click the checkbox in the "Total" section (toward the top of the table), in the "Unemployment Rate" row, in the

Labor Force Statistics from the Current Population Survey

Original Data Value													
Series ID:	LNU04000000												
Not Seasonally Adjusted													
Series title:	(Unadj) Unemployment Rate												
Labor force status:	Unemployment rate												
Type of data:	Percent or rate												
Age:	16 years and over												
Years:	2000 to 2010												
Year	Jan	Feb	Mar	Apr	May	Jun	Jul	Aug	Sep	Oct	Nov	Dec	Annual
2000	4.5	4.4	4.3	3.7	3.8	4.1	4.2	4.1	3.8	3.6	3.7	3.7	4.0
2001	4.7	4.6	4.5	4.2	4.1	4.7	4.7	4.9	4.7	5.0	5.3	5.4	4.7
2002	6.3	6.1	6.1	5.7	5.5	6.0	5.9	5.7	5.4	5.3	5.6	5.7	5.8
2003	6.5	6.4	6.2	5.8	5.8	6.5	6.3	6.0	5.8	5.6	5.6	5.4	6.0
2004	6.3	6.0	6.0	5.4	5.3	5.8	5.7	5.4	5.1	5.1	5.2	5.1	5.5
2005	5.7	5.8	5.4	4.9	4.9	5.2	5.2	4.9	4.8	4.6	4.8	4.6	5.1
2006	5.1	5.1	4.8	4.5	4.4	4.8	5.0	4.6	4.4	4.1	4.3	4.3	4.6
2007	5.0	4.9	4.5	4.3	4.3	4.7	4.9	4.6	4.5	4.4	4.5	4.8	4.6
2008	5.4	5.2	5.2	4.8	5.2	5.7	6.0	6.1	6.0	6.1	6.5	7.1	5.8
2009	8.5	8.9	9.0	8.6	9.1	9.7	9.7	9.6	9.5	9.5	9.4	9.7	9.3
2010	10.6	10.4	10.2	9.5	9.3	9.6	9.7	9.5	9.2				

EXHIBIT 5.3 Output of Bureau of Labor Statistics Unemployment Rate Report, Not Seasonally Adjusted

"Not seasonally adjusted" column. (We don't seasonally adjust the unemployment data for this purpose because the Google Trends data is not seasonally adjusted.)

6. Scroll to the bottom of the page and click the "Retrieve Data" button. You will come to another page that shows the unemployment rate data by year and by month, as shown in Exhibit 5.3. On that same page you will also see a "Download" icon to get the spreadsheet form of this data.

7. Combine the data into one spreadsheet in side-by-side columns so that each date has the relevant unemployment rate and search volume index for that month. Again, doing this can be a little tedious if you are not proficient with shortcut methods, so such a spreadsheet has already been prepared at www.pulsethenewscience.com. The spreadsheet will look like the example in Exhibit 5.4.

8. Now we can take a look at this combined data in a chart. First, I put these on the same scale so they can be seen right on top of each other. This will make how closely the data match more visually apparent. Simply create another column for each of the two columns where each number is divided by the number in the first row of the original column. Then make a line chart like the one shown in Exhibit 5.5. I won't go

Months/Year	BLS Unemployment Report	Search Volume Index: Unemployment
January-04	6.3	0.8
February-04	6	0.7
March-04	6	0.66
April-04	5.4	0.6
May-04	5.3	0.6
June-04	5.8	0.64
July-04	5.7	0.64
August-04	5.4	0.56
September-04	5.1	0.6
October-04	5.1	0.62
November-04	5.2	0.62
December-04	5.1	0.56
January-05	5.7	0.66
February-05	5.8	0.58
March-05	5.4	0.54
April-05	4.9	0.62

EXHIBIT 5.4   Suggested Arrangement for Combined BLS and Search Volume Data

into detail with the Excel steps for this but, again, just go to the example on the Web site if you want to see this work done already.

We will do more with this data, but now let's just step back and look at what we have. The correlation R between the search volume on the term "unemployment" and the official BLS data from January 2004 through August

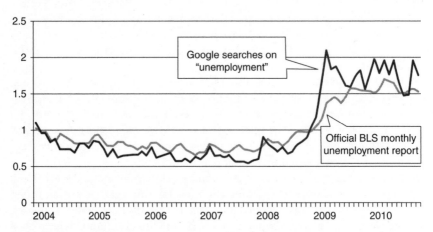

EXHIBIT 5.5   Relative Change in Google Search Volume Index and Unemployment (January 1, 2004 = 1)

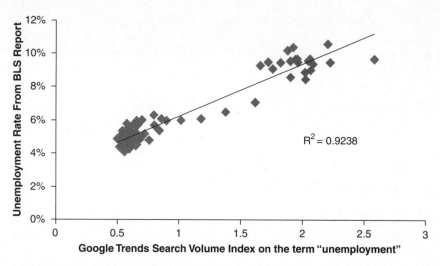

EXHIBIT 5.6 Official Unemployment versus Search Volume

2010 is about 0.96. The R^2, then, is about 0.92, which at first glance looks like an unbelievably tight relationship, especially given that the Google Trends data is available weeks before the official report. The completed spreadsheet at www.pulsethenewscience.com shows how this was calculated.

But the ability to predict unemployment month to month might not be as high as it first appears. This correlation is driven primarily by two clusters—one before mid-2008 and the other after mid-2008. So, the appearance of a high correlation might just be a function of two clusters of data spread apart by a considerable gap. To see what this looks like, we can plot the unemployment rate directly against the search volume as shown in Exhibit 5.6.

One way to gauge the month-to-month ability of searches to predict unemployment might be to look at these two clusters separately. That way, the apparent correlation is not just a function of one big jump in the data. If we look at all of the data after January 2009, the search volumes appear to lose all of their predictive value. The R^2 drops to 0.03. After that point in time, overall public attention may be driving a lot of the searches regardless of whether the people searching on the term are unemployed.

However, if we look at the period prior to 2009, the news reference volume is very low and for that period, the R is 0.83 and the R^2 is 0.7. These results are still fairly respectable. Furthermore, *the sudden spike in unemployment in January 2009 seems to have been predicted faster by search volumes than by the BLS*. Remember, the BLS data is plotted for the time period it measures, not when it was actually reported. The BLS reports data for a given time period three to five weeks later.

We can also go a little more advanced with our predictive modeling. So far, we looked at only a single variable to correlate to unemployment. But using the same data, we can make a slightly more sophisticated model. I created a model that uses four variables to predict unemployment:

1. The BLS reported unemployment for the previous month
2. The BLS reported unemployment for the period 12 months prior
3. The Google Trends Search Volume Index at the end of the reference week for the current month
4. The Google Trends Search Volume Index at the end of the reference week for the period 12 months earlier.

Using Excel, I created a multivariate model using four variables. This is something you can do if you download the Excel "Add-ins" for the Analysis Toolpack. If you click "data analysis" (which appears only after you install the Analysis Toolpack) and choose "Regression" from the list of analysis tools, you will see the fairly self-explanatory tool appear. (Refer to Excel help for more details if you need them.) I show the completed worksheet and chart for this multivariate model at www.pulsethenewscience.com.

This new model (see Exhibit 5.7) not only has a better fit to the entire data set, it also fits better within the two clusters. Now, we have an extraordinarily strong R^2 of 0.9741. Using this model, you can predict what the next BLS report will say—at least three weeks before the report is

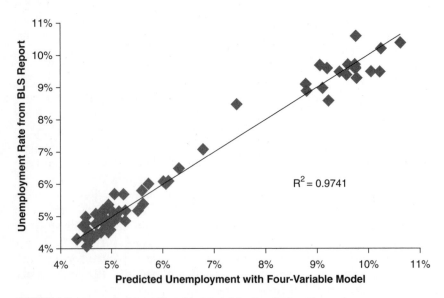

EXHIBIT 5.7 Improved Four-Variable Model for Predicting Unemployment

available—within an error of less than half of 1 percentage point of the unemployment rate.

More Searchology: The Body of Research Grows

It took two years after the initial research correlating search volumes to unemployment and influenza before the use of search volumes as a research tool began to get serious attention. The availability of Google Trends and Google Insights for search no doubt helped to spur further research. (Neither the first unemployment studies nor the first influenza studies had these tools at their disposal.[10]) The influenza study using data from Yahoo! helped to show that the tracking power of search volumes was not unique to Google but simply a fundamental consequence of the fact that, in the twenty-first century, people search the Internet for information about an illness before they report an illness to a doctor.

By 2009, the field some called "searchology"—using search volumes to predict various trends—was finally starting to take off as a legitimate area of research in several fields. And each article, like the previously mentioned one in *Nature*, added further credibility to the idea. Predicting trends in influenza and unemployment with search volumes still was a key area of research, but the research also expanded to include other topics in economics and health. And, in almost every study, researchers would find strong correlations. In some cases, the research would not only show results that predicted outcomes one or more weeks earlier but in some cases researchers would show searchology was more accurate than traditional methods. The flurry of research produced these results:

> April 2009: Hyunyoung Choi and Hal Varian, economists who work for Google, compared the search volume index from Google Trends to several areas of retail sales including travel, real estate, and auto sales. They found very strong correlations between auto and auto part sales and search volumes. They also found that statistical models that included both search volumes and historical sales data improved on models that used historical sales data alone. The authors noted that significant areas of improvement included "18% improvement in the predictions for 'Motor Vehicles and Parts' and the 12% improvement for 'New Housing Starts.'"[11] They referred to their results as "predicting the present" or "nowcasting" because they could not conclude that it was a forecast of trends, just that information about what is happing now is available more quickly with Google Trends than with official government statistics.
>
> June 2009: German researchers Nikolaos Askitas of the Institute for the Study of Labor and Klaus Zimmermann of the University

of Bonn used Google Insights for Search (www.google.com/insights/search/) to predict unemployment in Germany with four keywords (in German) associated with unemployment. One observation they made comparing the traditional methods to what I call the Pulse is particularly appropriate:

The Internet contains an enormous amount of information which, to our knowledge, classical econometrics has yet to appropriately tap into. Such information comes timely on a continual basis. It is particularly welcome at times of an economic crisis where the traditional flow of information is too slow to provide a proper basis for sound economic decisions. Not only has traditional (and typically official) statistical data a slow publication scheme, these data also do not reflect well the structural changes in the economy.[12]

July 2009: A study by Tanya Suhoy of the research department of the Bank of Israel shows that unemployment and several sectors of the economy correlate well with search volumes of certain keywords on Google Insights.[13] While Suhoy found that, unlike in the United States, Israeli search patterns show little or no correlation to purchases of automobiles, but purchases of home appliances and travel were found to be strongly correlated to search volumes. (The author chalks this up to possible differences in search behaviors between the two countries.) Suhoy also concluded that this method could have been used to predict the 2008 economic downturn.

July 2009: Choi and Varian, the Google researchers mentioned earlier, tested Google Trends search volumes against initial claims for unemployment benefits. Although it is a measure different from any used in the BLS report, it is related, and the authors found strong results similar to the example detailed in this chapter. They note that since new unemployment claims are a good indicator for past U.S. recessions, Google Trends data may predict coming recessions in addition to simply tracking current unemployment.

August 2009: Investigations conducted by researchers from the Institut National de la Santé et de la Recherche Médicale in Paris, France, showed how even more diseases have been tracked using Google Trends. Searches on outbreaks of chickenpox and acute diarrhea correlated well with (and were available faster than) data from the French sentinel network.

October/November 2009: Francesco D'Amuri and Juri Marcuccui of the Bank of Italy Economic Research Department confirmed the strong correlation between Google searches and the U.S. unemployment.[14,15] They concluded that models augmented with search volume data "outperform the traditional ones in predicting the monthly unemployment rate, even in most state-level forecasts and in comparison with the Survey of Professional Forecasters." *They recommended that search data be included in any unemployment forecasting model regardless of the country.*

November 2009: Torsten Schmidt and Simeon Vosen of the University of Ruhr, Germany, directly compared Google to survey-based methods of predicting consumer spending. They showed that Google search volumes *actually predict consumer spending better than traditional consumer confidence surveys* like the University of Michigan Consumer Sentiment Index and the Conference Board Consumer Confidence Index.[16] The Ruhr researchers also noted that

> . . . *the Google indicator is the only one to accurately indicate the turning point after consumption had reached its trough in December 2008.*

July 2010 (not yet published as of this writing; expected publication spring 2011): Haiyan Song of Hong Kong Polytechnic and Bing Pan of the College of Charleston showed that search volumes predict hotel demand. They concluded that tourists start planning travel about six weeks in advance by using Google searches.

So far, the research has overwhelmingly used Google, although some research has found similar results using Yahoo!. Google, after all, accounts for about two-thirds of all search volume (as of the spring of 2011). According to comScore, Yahoo! accounts for another 16%, and all the other search engines split the remainder. However, search volume alone doesn't account for the popularity of a search engine as a tool for socioeconomic research. Even the small percentage of searches answered by Ask.com or AOL.com amount to millions of searches a day. The difference in the amount of research being done with a particular search engine is probably more a function of data accessibility. That's something for Google's competitors to think about.

Another measure of our search patterns are the pages we actually visit. Although I haven't found any solid research on this, even a cursory view of the Alexa.com web traffic data (mentioned in Chapter 3) indicates the possibility that some high-traffic sites related to unemployment might be additional indicators of the unemployment rate. Traffic to the California's government services Web site (www.ca.gov) does seem to correlate with unemployment and economic trends in that state.

There are pros and cons to using direct Web site traffic counts compared to taking data directly from search tools. Visits to particular sites probably would be more volatile than generic searches on a topic, but that might allow for finer control search term context (e.g., people seeking unemployment benefits are looking for different sites than people seeking news stories about unemployment benefits). And while individual sites may spike for a number of reasons, large numbers of similar sites could be combined in a predictive model.

The list of research shown is by no means the end of this area of study. At the time of this writing, researchers were planning to investigate the predictive power of more keyword searches on an even wider variety of phenomena. As one researcher, Dr. Tanya Suhoy of the Bank of Israel, put it, this really is a "whole new field."

Caveats and Miscellaneous Considerations for Searchologists

Anyone using this sort of data to forecast reality has to be aware of some limitations and peculiar features of tools like Google Trends and Google Insights. In the help page on Google Insights, Google provides this caution for users of this data.

> *The data Trends produces may contain inaccuracies for a number of reasons, including data-sampling issues and a variety of approximations that are used to compute results. We hope you find this service interesting and entertaining, but you probably wouldn't want to write your PhD dissertation based on the information provided by Trends.*

Of course, as already stated, potential errors are themselves a hypothesis to be tested by the data. Clearly, these limitations did not stand in the way of strong correlations found by the long (and growing) list using this type of research. Remember that not only have people found this data convincing enough for PhD dissertations, the editors of *Nature* thought a study based on such data worthy of publication. The fact that inaccuracies may exist does not overturn the empirical findings when such a large number of data points are used over a long period of time in a variety of different forecasting problems. Bearing that in mind, there are a few things a person interested in this area of research might consider:

- *There appears to be a kind of Google "decay rate."* My assistants averaged the Google Trends data for about 100 randomly chosen, common English words, including "combine," "eating," and "triangle." The average showed a steady decrease in the search volume index for such common words. This finding might be an artifact of the data normalization method Google uses to adjust for changes in total search volume.

Google does not show actual search volumes for a keyword. If it did, virtually every search term would have a rapidly increasing search volume simply because the total number of people on the Internet continues to grow. Perhaps the growth in new search terms is enough to displace searches in common terms like these. Google decay is a small effect, amounting to about a 1% or 2% decay rate per year, on average. But considering this factor in a model might improve results of studies that compare several years of data.

- *Google may change historical data without notice.* I performed several studies looking for interesting correlation between Google search volumes and econometric data. When I would go back to get more recent data, I noticed in one instance that the historical search volume data had slightly changed. This may happen as Google "renormalizes" data, perhaps attempting to offset the Google decay. But in some cases an individual data point would be corrected or data for a given period might be lost. A searchologist should prepare for this by taking frequent downloads of the same term and comparing different versions of historical data.

- *Some types of search terms have clearly distinguishable search cycles.* Some searches follow a rhythm that repeats throughout the week or year, for example. Exhibit 5.8 shows the annual search cycles for shopping, travel, school, and jobs. These are averages of large numbers of search terms over many years. Unlike the Google decay rate, these are actually cycles that probably reflect real-world activities and therefore do not need to be controlled for when compared to real-world data. This information is more useful when determining categories of terms for particular applications. Among the curious features of this is that the search volumes of the terms "depression," "drugs," and "suicide" all fit the school cycle. This may simply be because students research these terms for classes—but apparently a lot of such searching is being undertaken.

- *Google uses server logs to determine a "best guess" on city and language.* So don't take location data for granted. Until the location data is validated against other real-world measurements (as all the previously mentioned studies have done), it, too, should be treated as an untested hypothesis.

- *Google Trends shows data daily for the most recent week, then only weekly aggregated data before that.* This temporary granularity shows a weekly pattern for the search term "unemployment." Most searching happens at the start of the calendar week then gradually declines until the end of the week. Since most of the search data for the week will be gathered in the first couple of days, this might add even a couple more days of lead time to economic trends.

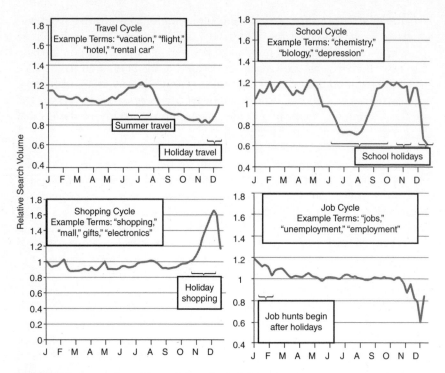

EXHIBIT 5.8   Examples of Annual Search Cycles

- *Google Insights is similar to Google Trends, but with some additional functionality, especially for locations.* Google Insights forecasts some search terms based on historical trends. It appears (just by looking, not through analysis) that these forecasts account for the kinds of annual cycles mentioned earlier. Google Insights also allows you to view an animation of a map indicating how search frequency (indicated by color codes) change over time. This tool is fun to experiment with as long as you remember the caveat about how Google estimates locations of searches.

- *Based on a simple visual inspection of some results from Google Trends and Google Insights, media reports clearly affect online behavior.* Unfortunately, Google does not produce this data in a form that can be exported to a spreadsheet, as it does with the search volume index. Further refinement of some models might be possible if references in the media could be used to adjust models using search volumes.

Using searches to track and predict trends in health and the economy is probably the most thoroughly researched area of the Pulse as well as the most easily accessible for the nontechnical person. Many times, right after I mention Google Trends to people who have not used it before, they start experimenting with it immediately. If they belonged to a big enough organization, they would try comparing search volume indices to sales of particular products or to economic trends of a particular industry or country.

Searchology is probably the easiest part of the Pulse and the most immediately gratifying. Next, we consider some areas of research that are either a bit more technical or have less easily accessible data.

Notes

1. J. Ginsberg, M.H. Mohebbi, R.S. Patel, L. Brammer, M.S. Smolinski, and L. Brilliant. "Detecting Influenza Epidemics Using Search Engine Query Data." *Nature.* 2009; 457: 1012–4.
2. N. Askitas, and K. Zimmermann. "Google Econometrics and Unemployment Forecasting." *Applied Economics Quarterly* 55, no. 2 (2009): 107–120.
3. comScore "comScore Releases December 2010 U.S. Search Engine Rankings" Press release last modified January 14, 2011.
4. G. Eysenbach, "Infodemiology: Tracking Flu-Related Searches on the Web for Syndromic Surveillance." *AMIA Annu Symp Proc.* 2006: 244–8.
5. P.M. Polgreen, Y. Chen, D.M. Pennock, and F.D. Nelson. "Using Internet Searches for Influenza Surveillance." *Clin Infect Dis.* 2008; 47:1443–8.
6. See Note 1.
7. J. Ortiz, et. al. "Does Google Influenza Tracking Correlate With Laboratory Tests Positive for Influenza?" *American Journal of Respiratory and Critical Care Medicine.*
8. M. Wenner. "Google Flu Trends Do Not Match CDC Data." *Popular Mechanics.* 17 May, 2010.
9. M. Ettredge, J. Gerdes, and G. Karuga. "Using Web-based Search Data to Predict Macroeconomic Statics." *Journal Commun ACM.* Vol. 48. 2005. 87–92.
10. Google Trends was available prior to the publication of Eysenbach's work, but it was not available for the 2004/2005 flu season he was studying.
11. C. Hyunyoung, and H. Varian. "Predicting the Present With Google Trends." Google, Inc. International Paper, April 10, 2009. 18.
12. See Note 2.
13. T. Suhoy, "Query Indices and a 2008 Downturn: Israeli Data." *Bank of Israel Discussion Paper.* No. 2009.06, July 2009.
14. F. D'Amuri, "Predicting Unemployment In Short Samples With Internet Job Search Query Data." Bank of Italy Economic Research Department. October 2009.

15. F. D'Amuri and J. Marcucci, "'Google It!' Forecasting the U.S. Unemployment Rate with a Google job Search Index," Bank of Italy Economic Research Department, November 2009.

16. T. Schmidt, and S. Vosen. "Forecasting Private Consumption: Survey-Based Indicators vs. Google Trends." *Ruhr Economic Papers* no. 155. November 2009.

CHAPTER 6

"Friend" as a Verb

As we studied social networks more deeply, we began to think of them as a kind of human super-organism. They grow and evolve. All sorts of things flow and move within them. This super-organism has a structure and a function, and we became obsessed with understanding both.
— Nicholas Christakis, *Connected*, 2009

Studying the connections we make among ourselves is a powerful tool for understanding what is happening in the Pulse. If studying society means studying social connections and their effects, then we've never had as many powerful tools and so much recorded information available. Using this information could be a big payoff for measuring the Pulse. The study of social networks has shown that not only can flu outbreaks be forecasted faster (even faster than search patterns alone) but so can depression, obesity, alcoholism, sleep deprivation, and happiness.

Even gossip, fads, technology adoption, and political movements could be modeled and forecasted using information about social networks. Some researchers are applying this data to the study of how to disrupt terrorist networks. If you are attempting to inoculate a population against a virus, take down an organized crime network, or forecast political opinions, a random sample of the entire population is not nearly as useful as sample that is biased toward highly connected individuals.

Unlike research done using Google or Yahoo! searches, this part of the Pulse is really about a possible connection between research using traditional research methods and that using new nontraditional sources of data. Computational social science (CSS) existed well before Facebook, MySpace, LinkedIn, or other online social networks. Consequently, there has been a lot of good scientific research in this field, but it was usually based on large surveys or data that is not publicly available (e.g., databases of emails and text messages). That meant that only the best-funded studies had significant amounts of data, even for studies even as recent as 2010. In fact, most of the academic research shown in this chapter is not from

Facebook or any other online social networking service, but from traditional survey methods.

There is, of course, a lot of data in publicly available forms, but it has not been the target of much scientific research. This is a major unrealized opportunity since at least a quarter of all Internet users worldwide—over half a billion people—are using some kind of online social networking service. Chapter 3 showed how Facebook now accounts for the single largest use of time on the Internet. Since so many people are spending so much time on it, it should be a great source of social data.

We look at two issues in this chapter: what has been discovered in the study of social networks using traditional data collection methods and then what sort of data could be available from a source like Facebook. But first, let's introduce the basic concept of social networks as a theory.

How Do Social Networks Matter?

The original sense of CSS was really about simulations of networks of people. Computer models showing connections between (mostly hypothetical) individuals would be used to explore abstract characteristics of the system. Technically, the study of these networks is called *graph theory*, but it's not about the graphs of mathematical functions you might normally associate with math. In this context, a *graph* is a set of connected things. The things being connected are called *nodes* or *vertices*, and the connections between the nodes are sometimes called the *edges* of the graph. See Exhibit 6.1 for an example of such a network.

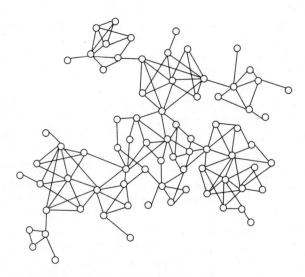

EXHIBIT 6.1   Example of a (Relatively Simple) Network

Networks represent many kinds of real-world objects. Networks of nodes and their connections in general could represent the connections of computers, roads, electrical circuits, and any other set of things that are linked to each other. Social networks (our focus here) represent sets of people and their connections via family, friends, business, or other associations. Networks have been studied both in a pure mathematical sense and as an empirical science.

As networks grow in size, they become mathematically complex very quickly. This is why computational methods have been so important in the study of networks. In theory, the number of possible connections in a network is equal to $(n^2 - n)/2$, where n is the number of nodes in the network. The maximum number of connections would exist only if every node were connected directly to every other node. Ten people would have only 45 possible connections, and 1,000 people would have about half a million possible connections. Real-world networks contain just a fraction of the possible connections, and in social networks in particular, the connections are not just random or uniform. Here are a few features of social networks:

- In a network of people, there is usually some degree of *homophily*, a tendency to make connections with people with similar attributes.
- Some people will have a large number of connections, and some will have very few.
- One consequence of homophily is *transitivity*. That is, if John is friends with Bill and Ben, then Ben and Bill are a bit more likely to be friends with each other than if they had no other friends in common.
- Homophily and transitivity tend to create clusters where the people in that cluster tend to have many connections within and fewer outside of the cluster. One measure of a cluster around a single person is his or her *network density*. This is the proportion of connections among a person's friends compared to the number of possible connections between that number of individuals.
- In some cases, networks can be modeled to give the connections themselves more descriptive complexity. The connections between people can have features including whether it is a family, friend, or business. Some connections can be stronger and may have a much more active level of interaction than others. Connections can have both a direction and a magnitude, such as in the direction of authority implied by an organizational chart or social influence of a popular person.
- A measure of a node's position in a network is its *betweenness centrality*. This measure quantifies how often this node (i.e., person) is in the path between two other nodes in the network. A node or person with a high centrality can have a lot of friends or can simply be the bridge between two big clusters.

- Some things that move through networks can be considered a type of "contagion," or some kind of change that one node transmits to another via a connection. A contagion can be literal, as in a flu virus. But it also can be a bit of gossip, a new fad, political opinions, or panic about the economy.
- On average, the nodes connected to a randomly chosen node will have more connections than the initial, randomly chosen node. In other words, your friends have more friends than you do.[1] What first seems like a paradox is actually quite logical. By definition, you are friends with no one who has no friends. You are less likely to be among the friends of people with very few friends and more likely to be among the friends of people with lots of friends. (This quirky feature of networks has a practical consequence you will see shortly.)

The complexity of social networks is the reason we need to rely on computational methods to simulate how ideas and other contagions travel through a network. The number of combinations of ways that things can travel through a network grows much faster than even the number of possible connections can grow. In order to visualize such a system changing over time, we have to resort to unrealistically simple networks, as shown in Exhibit 6.2. In this simulation, there is randomness involved, just as in the real world. I show a set of nodes where, in each iteration, each node has a 50% chance of "catching" something from each contaminated node it is connected to. A large number of simulations have to be run in order to work out the odds that a given node will catch the contagion by a certain iteration. For more realistic (i.e., much bigger) networks, the complexity grows quickly.

But as complicated as graph theory can be, it is considered a fairly well-defined problem in mathematical circles. Additional mathematical properties and laws have been discovered, and very elaborate simulations of networks such as electrical power distribution grids have been put to practical use for some time. Applying this to people is a key challenge of CSS. Fortunately, some researchers have broken a lot of ground in this area.

The Dynamic Duo of Social Connections: Two Leaders in Practical Network Research

Social science may be seen as having two eras: before network theory and after. Massive surveys of the twentieth century that tried to measure and forecast the spread of affluence, political opinions, and health conditions might report the percentage of people who had a condition or responded a

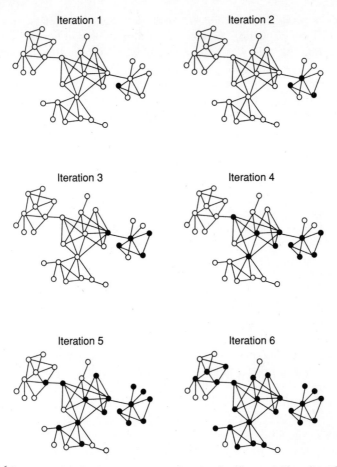

EXHIBIT 6.2 Example of a Contagion (e.g., Gossip, the Flu, etc.) Traveling through a Network

Contagion rate is 50% per connection per iteration

certain way on a survey. But the people's network connections were generally ignored. Given the influence of social networks on all these phenomena, it now seems that studying such things without network information is like studying chemistry without knowledge of the elements or studying geology without knowledge of tectonic plates.

There is a lot of research in the area of social networks, but for a quick introduction into the field, Nicholas Christakis and James Fowler are the best place to start. Christakis is a professor of medicine and of sociology at Harvard. Fowler is at the University of California, San Diego and, like Christakis, he is a professor of both medicine and sociology. They are two of the most prolific researchers in social networks. They have coauthored at least a dozen papers on the role of social networks in health as well as a book on the topic that was chosen as an official Oprah's Book Club pick.[2] *Science* magazine called these two thought leaders the "dynamic duo" of this emerging field—a field that is emerging, in a large part, due to their efforts.

Both were among the 15 authors of the 2008 *Science* article that discussed how the key obstacle to growth in CSS is the lack of data. However, the authors of the article had already foreseen the solution. They recognized that in order for research like theirs to really take off, they would have to tap into the massive and relatively recent sources of data available from online social media. In fact, by the time they coauthored the article in *Science,* they were already beginning to investigate how online social networks could provide a solution.

Christakis says he recalls the moment when he started to recognize the relevance of networks in healthcare; it was during a call from a stranger, a friend of a husband of the daughter of a patient of his. In the mid-1990s, he was working as a doctor in the hospice care ward of the University of Chicago Medical Center. An old woman was being cared for by an exhausted daughter. This exhaustion led to depression, which affected the mental and physical health of her husband. The friend of the husband experienced his own depression because of his friend's depression, and that friend called Dr. Christakis to tell him of the situation. Prior to that, Christakis had already studied the health impact of immediate family members on each other. But after this call he began to see that if one person could affect another, then the other person could affect yet another, and so on. Social networks were the key to understanding this critical healthcare issue.

Many of the studies Christakis and Fowler conducted were based on a traditional, massive survey like the Framingham Heart Study (FHS). FHS has been a great source of health and interpersonal data gathered since 1948. What was then called the National Heart Institute recruited over 5,000 people from Framingham, Massachusetts, to be subjects for a study of detailed health data from people in a single community. Now under the direction of the National Heart, Lung and Blood Institute and Boston University, over 12,000 inhabitants of Framingham are closely tracked in this study. This massive data set has produced not only many important health studies but many careers in health research as well.

It was with this massive data set that Christakis and Fowler—sometimes with other researchers—were able to investigate the spread of various health problems among connected people. Obesity and smoking were the first two of the health-related issues they studied. Using decades of data from the FHS records, they were able to show that if you are obese or a smoker, you are probably more likely to have friends who are obese or smokers.

The correlation could be partly due to birds of a feather flocking together, but that can't be the only explanation since often the change in weight, for example, happens *after* an association. Obese people and thin people often have different activities. Regular pizza and beer parties as opposed to playing tennis are activities that eventually lead to different health outcomes. Association with one group rather than the other may lead to peer pressure to join them in their activities, which often leads to shared health results. The same is true with the activities of smokers.

A more subtle possible explanation is that what is transmitted from one person to another is actually the norm of what is acceptable or even attractive. Being around thinner people may cause a heavier person to feel self-conscious while associations with similarly overweight people may cause a person to perceive his or her weight as normal. Whatever the combination of causes behind why we tend to emulate friends, Christakis and Fowler were able to determine that these conditions spread through a social network just like a virus.

Using the FHS data, Fowler and Christakis continued to investigate other phenomena to see if they, too, might spread like a virus. In this line of research, 2008 to 2010 were particularly prolific years for both of them. Their research with the FHS data showed how happiness, loneliness, depression, and other emotional states along with alcoholism spread through networks in a similar fashion. In each case, they observed that the "infection" could spread through a network person to person like any contagion. See Table 6.1 for a summary of their research from 2008 through 2010.

There were some differences between these networks and the spread of an actual virus. First, there is no "patient zero" to whom all obesity, smoking, or happiness could be traced. The conditions would randomly appear for several people throughout the network, and the condition might spread from there. Another difference is that the "infected" and "uninfected" often formed relatively stable clusters. The contagious condition would not necessarily continue to spread nor would it eventually go away.

In other studies, Fowler and Christakis used different data sources to study adolescent health or social dynamics of college students. One study showed how sleep behavior spread through networks of adolescents.[3] In another case, they performed a lab experiment with 240 students showing how cooperative behavior cascades through a network.[4] It seemed that just about anything wherever the behavior of one person has some influence on the behavior of another, modeling the network would be critical in understanding the phenomenon. But in one particular study based on a survey of their own design, they found that understanding social networks provided something that could be particularly useful public health and businesses alike: They could forecast the future of crowds better.

TABLE 6.1   Selected Research by Nicholas Christakis, James Fowler, and other Co-authors

Year	Study Title	Data Source*
2008	"The Collective Dynamics of Smoking in a Large Social Network"[i]	FHS
	"Tastes, Ties, and Time: A New (Cultural, Multiplex, and Longitudinal) Social Network Dataset Using Facebook.com"[ii]	CS, FB
	"The Taste for Privacy: An Analysis of College Student Privacy Settings in an Online Social Network"[iii]	CS, FB
	"The Dynamic Spread of Happiness in a Large Social Network: Longitudinal Analysis Over 20 Years in the Framingham Heart Study"[iv]	FHS
2009	"Alone in the Crowd: The Structure and Spread of Loneliness in a Large Social Network"[v]	FHS
	"Social Network Determinants of Depression"[vi]	FHS
2010	"Infectious Disease Modeling of Social Contagion in Networks"[vii]	T
	"Cooperative Behavior Cascades in Human Social Networks"[viii]	CS
	"The Spread of Sleep Behavior Influences Drug Use in Adolescent Social Networks"[ix]	AH
	"The Spread of Alcohol Consumption Behavior in a Large Social Network"[x]	FHS
	"Emotions as Infectious Diseases in a Large Social Network"[xi]	FHS
	"Social Network Sensors for Early Detection of Contagious Outbreaks"[xii]	CS

*Source of data for the studies: FHS = Framingham Heart Study; AH= University of NC Add Health database; CS = surveys of college students; FB = Facebook; T = theoretical

[i] N. Christakis and J. Fowler. *New England Journal of Medicine 358*, no. (21):2249–58 (May 22, 2008).

[ii] K. Lewis, J. Kaufman, M. Gonzalez, A. Wimmer, and N. Christakis. *Social Networks* (2008).

[iii] K. Lewis, J. Kaufman, and N. A. Christakis. *Journal of Computer-Mediated Communications* 14, no. 1 (2008):79–1000.

[iv] J. H. Fowler and N. A. Christakis. *British Medical Journal 337*, no. a2338 (2008):1–9.

[v] J. T. Cacioppo, J. H. Fowler, and N. A. Christakis. (December 1, 2008). http://ssrn.com/abstract=1319108

[vi] J. N. Rosenquist, J .H. Fowler, and N. A. Christakis. *Molecular Psychiatry*, Vol. aop, No. current (March 16, 2010).

[vii] A. L. Hill, D. G. Rand, M. A. Nowak, N. A. Christakis. *PLoS Computational Biology* 6(11) (2010).

[viii] J. H. Fowler and N. A. Christakis. *Proceedings of the National Academy of Sciences* 107, no. 12 (March 2010):533438.

[ix] S. C. Mednick, N. A. Christakis, and J. H. Fowler. *PLoS One* 5(3) (March 19, 2010): e9775.

[x] J. N. Rosenquist, J. Murabito, J. H. Fowler, and N. A. Christakis. *Ann Intern Med* 152(7): 426–33 (April 6, 2010).

[xi] A. L. Hill, D. G. Rand, M. A. Nowak, and N. A. Christakis. *Proceedings of the Royal Society B: Biological Sciences* (July 7, 2010).

[xii] N. A. Christakis and J. H. Fowler. *PloS One* 5(9) (2010): e12948.

Forecasting the Crowd

In the fall of 2009, Christakis and Fowler conducted an influenza study by tracking 744 Harvard students and details of their social networks.[5] They recruited subjects for their study by asking an initially randomly chosen set of students to nominate friends. Many of the nominations were overlaps with other nominated students, and some were students who were already in the randomly chosen set. This method ensured that the students in the study would be part of an interconnected network. The student volunteers agreed to regular inspections of their health conditions.

As Fowler and Christakis observed the flu moving through the network, they noticed that persons nominated by friends tended to have higher centrality in the network. This is the "your friends have more friends than you do" effect mentioned earlier. A nominated person will, on average, have more friends than the person nominating him or her; this tends to create a higher centrality for the nominated person. Since the nominated people connect to more people than a randomly selected person, they acted like a kind of early warning sensor for the network. By tracking the right people, Fowler and Christakis could predict the flu outbreaks significantly earlier than methods that ignored social network effects.

The nominated friends had a flu cycle similar to that of everyone else. Cases of the flu rose quickly at first, peaked at some point, and then eventually declined. The difference was that their higher centrality caused them to experience this cycle *two weeks before the rest of the students*. Exhibit 6.3 shows the peak of the flu incidents for both the randomly selected group and the group of nominated friends.

This effect can be leveraged in other ways. Christakis has noted that the effectiveness of a vaccination program could be greatly increased by randomly selecting people and then asking those people to nominate friends. Vaccinating a randomly selected set of 30% of the population would have very little effect on an epidemic. However, vaccinating the nominated friends of the randomly selected 30% has the same effect as vaccinating a randomly selected 90% of the population. Since there are usually limited doses of vaccines during critical periods of flu outbreaks, any tactic with such a highly leveraged effect cannot be ignored.

Given the wide range of phenomena which behave like a contagion, this time-shifted effect of the high-centrality nodes could be powerful in many ways. Gossip, fads, technology adoption, and ideas often have shapes like the flu cycle. There is a period of accelerating growth, culminating in a peak, and then a decline. In theory, more central nodes should experience the same cycle, just earlier than the rest of the population. Think of the trend-setting in-crowd always being a step or two ahead of the rest on fashion, culture, and technology. And, as marketers have long known, if you want

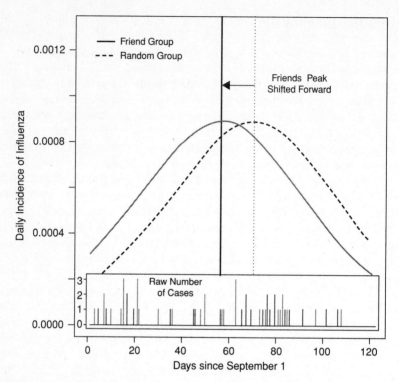

EXHIBIT 6.3   The Friend Shift Observed by Christakis and Fowler

Source: N. A. Christakis and J. H. Fowler. "Social Network Sensors for Early Detection of Contagious Outbreaks." *PLoS One 5*, no. 9 (September 2010)

to advertise a product, seeking out high-centrality trend setters is always a good idea.

Social Networks in the Pulse

As critical as this research is, it is not yet the Pulse. Unlike the search pattern research in Chapter 5, this research was not based on real-time, publicly available data from large populations. The data Christakis and Fowler used for most of their research was the sort that the average person would not have access to. Nor did Christakis and Fowler attempt to compare their findings to macro-trends like unemployment or regional flu outbreaks like the Google and Yahoo! research did. Some of their studies focused on networks in a single college dormitory; even the largest data set represented only a single and not particularly large town in Massachusetts. Some of the data was longitudinal—that is, tracked over time—but it was not actually real-time. After careful analysis, Christakis and Fowler could see only in retrospect what was going on, and the data was not the type that could translate immediately into a useful predictive tool.

Still, these two researchers were also breaking ground on the use of Facebook as a source of data for analysis. They performed two studies that relied on data that required the permission of both Facebook and the colleges—one study focused on privacy settings and the other looked at the broader social structure. Each study used only college students as subjects, and both had just over 1,600 students participating. Surely, a college is an environment that has different social characteristics from most of the rest of the world. Also, this research was of an exploratory nature about the structure of Facebook, not about trying to predict macro-trends.

A source like Facebook could help make the connection between the prediction of real-world macro-trends and the research of Fowler and Christakis. Given the amount of data half a billion people seem to be willing to divulge about themselves and their connections, a source like this will be a critical piece of the Pulse. So let's take a look at what Facebook can do and what might be needed to make it a scientifically validated tool for forecasting macro-trends.

The practicality of using social networks like Facebook for the Pulse depends quite a lot on users' privacy settings and the size and insularity of their networks. The more information users share, the more information there is available about them and their networks, and the more we can use for tracking the Pulse. If, in addition to openness about friend lists, users have enough friends and their friends are not too insular (i.e., do not have a large network density), then large parts of an entire online social network could be mapped out.

I wanted to see if it might have been feasible for Christakis and Fowler to conduct their research with a much larger group by only using data directly available from Facebook (i.e., without using any data that would require special permission of Facebook or its users). I sampled 1,312 accounts on Facebook using two different random name generators. (You can find several online with a search.) I made no attempt to measure whether the names had any "Western" bias, but there were plenty of examples of ethnically diverse names in the list.

My assistants entered the randomly generated names into the search tool for Facebook. They generally found several people to whom that name could refer. I asked them to select three (or, if fewer than three were available, as many as were available) and note whether they displayed their friends. Three of *their* friends were selected using a random number generator to select the page number and friend position on the friends list. Since there were overlaps and some who had only one or two friends, this

Those who display: (no public display may be due to privacy settings or failure to post data)	Group 1 (1,312 samples): Randomly selected from Facebook	Error (+/-)	Group 2 (2,691 samples): Randomly selected from friends of Group 1	Error (+/-)
Friends List	69%	2.1%	74%	1.4%
Relationship Status	25%	2.8%	28%	2.0%
Wall (where comments are posted by user or friends)	41%	3.2%	35%	2.1%
Likes	55%	3.2%	65%	2.1%
Friends of same Group 1 person who were friends of each other			13.1%	2.0%

EXHIBIT 6.4   Summary of Survey from Facebook

added 2,691 who were friends of the first group. Here is a summary of what I found compared to the studies using college students (Exhibit 6.4 also summarizes the results):

- First, I looked at privacy settings. In Facebook privacy settings, you can decide to display friend connections, profile information, and even your daily "updates" (the comments on your "wall"). In each of nine different areas of information, privacy can be set to "Everyone," "Friends of Friends," or "Friends only." Or the access can be more finely customized by specifying individuals who have access to the data. Of the 1,312 people we randomly selected, 31% chose not to publicly display their friend lists to everyone. This is a higher percentage than the Facebook study done by Christakis and Fowler (15%). College students may simply be less guarded about social information. This study was done in the fall of 2010 and, since then, Facebook has changed policies to improve privacy. But a subsequent check of the data with a smaller sample indicates that the percentage who choose not to reveal friends has not increased and may have in fact gone down.
- Then I looked at the general structure of the networks of randomly selected people. I found that my initially randomly selected group tended to have more friends than the group of college students: 251 versus 109. This could be because college social networks are more insular, or it could be because the average number of friends per person has grown in the two years since Christakis and Fowler's initial study.

- I also found that a random sample of all Facebook users shows a lower network density than that of the college students: 13% versus 22%. That is, the college students participating in Christakis and Fowler's research had friends more likely to be friends of each other than would the friends of a randomly selected person from Facebook. We expected this in Christakis and Fowler's research, however, since all the friends of a person in their study were limited to people who were also college students at the same institution.

- My survey confirms the "your friends have more friends than you do" effect. In our sample of randomly selected names from Facebook, 908 of the initially selected names shared their friends, and they averaged 251 friends per person. But a randomly selected set of *their* friends who shared their friend list had 433 friends per person on average.

- A corollary of the "your friends have more friends than you do" law of networks seems to be "your friends are more likely to share their friends than you are." This may not be a mathematical law like the first rule, but it does appear to be an empirical fact. Whereas 31% of the randomly selected list of Facebook users did not display their friends for public viewing, only 26% of the friends of that group did the same. (The margins of error are much smaller than the difference between the groups.) Maybe this is because people who share their friends are more likely to be friends with people who share friends. Or maybe people who have lots of friends are the kinds of people who are more likely to share friends.

- A significant percentage of users also publicly share their "wall" postings on Facebook (41%), their relationship status (25%), and their "Likes" (55%). Curiously, while the share of those who display their likes publicly goes up for the friends of the first group, the percentage of friends who share their wall publicly goes down. (Do people with more friends worry more about what gets posted on their wall to the general public?)

So far, it looks like the publicly available information for the general population is, if anything, more useful for the Pulse than a study of college students might first indicate. While the average Facebook user seems a bit more guarded about sharing friend lists than college students, this is more than offset by the higher number of friends per person and the fact that users in general have less insular friends than college students. And considering that Facebook has a half billion users, apparently tens of millions share their detailed wall posts, likes, and even relationship status.

LinkedIn, a popular social networking service used primarily for business connections, gives us some additional insight into some properties of social networks with its "network statistics" page. (As a business-focused service, it doesn't call relationships "friends," just "connections.") This page simply lists how many connections you have, how many are "two degrees away," and how many are "three degrees away." "Two degrees away" refers to those who are connected to those you are connected to, but LinkedIn counts each person only once. In other words, if two of your friends have another person in common as a friend, that person is counted only once between them. "Three degrees away" refers to connections of connections of connections.

My connections on LinkedIn are a modest 170 (I don't manage my account closely), but my connections two degrees away are listed as "88,500+," and the connections three degrees away are shown as "6,497,400+." The total is then shown as 6,586,100+ since both sets are unique individuals and have no overlap between them. The numbers indicate that while my connections add over 520 unique, nonoverlapping connections per person, the connections of *their* connections only add another 73 or so unique connections per person. Since there were just over 80 million users of LinkedIn when I checked these numbers, those 6.5 million contacts up to three degrees from me can connect to no more than 12 new unique contacts per person before we branch out to entire population of users. If my connections three degrees removed would not nearly touch all 80 million LinkedIn users, then most likely four degrees of separation would be enough.

Data showing the number of connections two and three places removed is not immediately available on Facebook, but it tells us something about connections in all social networks. The population of Facebook and LinkedIn are probably not a large number of unconnected networks, each comprising only a small minority of the population. Instead, it is more likely that the majority of users in a network can be connected to the majority of other users (although several degrees removed), even if we are restricted only to those who choose to publicly display their connections to others.

There are two principles of measurement I like to reiterate for my clients, and they seem particularly appropriate here. You have more data than you think, and you need less data than you think. In that spirit, here are a few other miscellaneous issues to consider when tracking the Pulse on social network sites:

- All of this data is available through scrapers and crawlers but *not* the Facebook Application Program Interface (API) known as the Graph API. With most scrapers and APIs, if you can see it on the page, you can access it in an automated way. To download data from Facebook, the Graph API still requires explicit permission from the Facebook user even if that data is already publicly shared by the user.
- We have the option of using "picture friends," a device Christakis and Fowler used to measure the strength of a connection based on pictures

they post of each other. The idea is that if two people post pictures about each other, then they probably have a closer relationship than people who do not.

- Whether we use picture friends to measure the strength of connections or not, we may not need to be concerned with whether the connections on Facebook or LinkedIn are mostly meaningless "one-click friends." One study showed that fewer than 1% of friendships on Facebook are purely online acquaintances.[5] Most connections on Facebook simply reinforce existing offline relationships.[6]

- The strength of connections can also be inferred from the propagation of interests and preferences. Enough of the network can be filled in to determine the direction of influence in networks of people. If we notice that "causes," "tastes," or "likes" of some people tend to be adopted by others, perhaps we can measure a level of influence for that person. Then perhaps those who influence others could be good leading indicators of other interests and preferences.

- We don't really need the picture of the whole network to get use out of network data for practical forecasting. The research of Christakis and Fowler already showed that simply tracking the friends of randomly selected people will forecast the crowd. Or perhaps we could limit tracking to people who have a certain number of friends or picture friends.

- Some heavy-hitter software is entering this space. The statistical software firm SAS released its Social Media Analytics (SMA) tool in April 2010. Power tools like this will make all of this analysis much more practical for the average manager. SMA is a more specialized extension of SAS Social Media Analytics based on a successful use of this tool in fraud detection. In 2008, Los Angeles County used SAS Social Media Analytics to analyze networks of people on public assistance. It could detect collusive fraud rings with an 85% accuracy and saved the county over $6.8 million a year. Because of its genesis in fraud detection, the primary focus of the marketing of SMA seems to be in that area. But as a general analytical tool, it would be useful on any research in social networks.

This is encouraging for those who want to track the Pulse. Using online social networks for the Pulse is certainly a larger effort than what is required for tracking search behavior, as we did in the last chapter. But it gets at an entirely different level of data that could be even more insightful than search data alone. The search volume index generated by Google does not tell us where searchers are in their network and how they might influence other people. If we can track something about what people do *together* by tracking where they are in a network, then we could be in a position to forecast waves of fads, opinions, anxieties, and more that would otherwise not be apparent without seeing the network.

The practical use of social networks does not have to wait. In the field of national security in particular, analysis of social networks is already being put to use. The Department of Defense uses social network analysis (SNA) or dynamic network analysis (DNA) to analyze the effects of targeting individuals in a terrorist network. The idea is to identify targets who would maximize the disruption of the network and to try to predict how the network would adjust to the damage. I did not get permission to divulge details of some of my conversations with intelligence-related researchers prior to the publication of this book. However, some publicly available information indicates that there is a serious, ongoing effort to develop the use of SNA for defense. In fact, it was already used with some effectiveness in determining who would be the likely successors to terrorist leaders when they are eliminated. The National Security Agency, the Office of Naval Research, the Central Intelligence Agency and the Defense Advanced Research Projects Agency and other agencies have all jumped into SNA with both feet.

Of course, much of the information gathered by the intelligence community that would be used to build detailed social network models is beyond the reach of the rest of us. The social network analysis of Al Qaeda is obviously not based on surveys of terrorists or a download of their Facebook connections. There is, however, one particular application of SNA within the intelligence community that builds on publicly available information: It builds social networks based on blogs.

SNA based on blogs involves the analysis of unstructured text, and it requires a different kind of analysis than what we have seen so far. In some ways, the analysis of millions of micro-blog comments on Twitter (tweets) is also a social network since it allows for individuals to follow the tweets of other individuals. In other ways, the analysis of text is much more developed, practical, and scientifically validated to predict real-world events than social network analysis alone. Next, we will discuss recent research showing how what we say in blogs, customer reviews, and tweets actually generates a Pulse.

Notes

1. S. Feld. "Why Your Friends Have More Friends Than You Do." *American Journal of Sociology* 96, no. 6 (May 1991).
2. N. Christakis and J. Fowler. *Connected: the Surprising Power of Our Social Networks and How They Change Our Lives*, Little, Brown and Company, 2009.
3. S.C. Mednick, N.A. Christakis, and J.H. Fowler. "The Spread of Sleep Behavior Influences Drug Use in Adolescent Social Networks." *PLoS One* 5, no. (3): (March 2010): e9775.

4. J.H. Fowler and N.A. Christakis. "Cooperative Behavior Cascades in Human Social Networks," *PNAS: Proceedings of the National Academy of Sciences*. Vol. 107, no. (9). March 2010. 5334–5338.

5. A. Mayer and S.L. Puller. "The Old Boy (and Girl) Network: Social Network Formation on University Campuses." *Journal of Public Economics* 92 (2008): 329–347.

6. D.M. Boyd and N.B. Ellison. "Social Network Sites: Definition, History, and Scholarship." *Journal of Computer-Mediated Communication* 13, (2007).

CHAPTER 7

What We Say Online Matters

just setting up my twttr
> —First Twitter message, Jack Dorsey, CEO, cofounder of
> Twitter, March 21, 2006, 9:50 PM PST

65 million tweets composed per day represent a detailed, real-time trace of the collective thoughts and feelings of a significant fraction of the population—potentially offering valuable information to everyone from politicians to advertisers to social researchers.
> —Alan Mislove, developer of the Pulse of the Nation, August 2010

There was a period in human history, just prior to the advent of the telephone and the television, when most people wrote letters. The literacy rate was high enough by the nineteenth and early twentieth centuries that a large amount of history of that period could be gathered from letters and diaries. But writing letters and journals began to decline—even as literacy continued to rise—with the advent of the telephone. After the telephone came into common use, we didn't have to write to communicate over a distance.

Now we have a resurgence in written communication, which also happens to be much more accessible than paper letters. Some of our communications are private, but a share of it is public pronouncements—blogs, product reviews, tweets. Some of these communications are anonymous, but many use the identifiable real names of the people who stated them. Even location and other details are sometimes provided.

Blogs, product reviews, comments to friends on Facebook, and Twitter are some of the ways we leave our footprints in a highly unstructured text form. Using these as a source of data for social science research is messy, but we do tend to use certain words more frequently depending on mood, our worries about the economy, and whether we liked a particular product or movie. With over 130 million blogs on the Internet and the users of

Twitter posting over 100 million tweets per day (at the beginning of 2011), sample size is not a problem.

It was only 1999—a lifetime ago in Internet time—when the term "web log" morphed into "blog." According to the blog-tracking site Technorati, there were 500,000 blogs by the fall of 2003; in the next three years, that number grew by a factor of 100. The appearance of "micro-blogs" would add another burst of growth to blogging when Twitter was founded in 2006.

Twitter used the Short Message Service (SMS)—originally designed for texting between phones—to post micro-blogs called "tweets" of no more than 140 characters in length. This new service made blog posts—at least of the very short variety—feasible to do from mobile phones. By January 2009, the number of tweets exceeded the number of all other blogs. As of 2010, there were over 50 times as many posts on Twitter as on all other blogs combined. According to Techcrunch.com, Twitter had only about 5,000 tweets per day in 2007 but grew by a factor of almost 30 every year since. In addition, the Pulse includes wall posts on Facebook, product reviews on eBay or Amazon, and all the other places where our thoughts are recorded for posterity.

According to Twitter, 90% of tweets are public and Twitter has been in the lead in making its data available for analysis. It has multiple Application Program Interfaces (APIs) that can give direct access to the data, including the Firehose API, which can give developers real-time access to all 100+ million tweets each day. Access to data like this is relevant because the tweets are talking about something that matters. Nineteen percent of all tweets mention a brand.[1] And, as you will see shortly, tweets can even predict the economy.

An Introduction to Analyzing Buzz: Counting Tweets Predicts Movie Box Office Receipts

Perhaps the simplest way to get a handle on the overall buzz in a vast string of blog posts is simply to count the frequency of use of particular words. Over a four-month period starting in November 2009, Sitaram Asur and Bernardo Huberman of HP Labs in Palo Alto, California, analyzed a large sample of tweets that mentioned one of 24 different movies being released during that time. They work in HP's "social computing lab" (a type of lab you may see more often as these concepts evolve), and their goal was to see if this form of social media could predict movie box office receipts.

Huberman had already worked on several papers regarding social networks (the topic of Chapter 6), but mostly from a theoretical point of view. He investigated how opinions move through a crowd and how public opinions form, but only with simulations devoid of real-world data. Still, such an exercise is always useful because having a sound theory is half of science. The other half is using the theory to predict outcomes with real data.

Using a Twitter API called the Search API, Asur and Huberman extracted 2.89 million tweets from 1.2 million unique users—each tweet mentioning one of the 24 movie titles. They did encounter some of the challenges that researchers analyzing large volumes of text often run into. For example, it was impractical for them to attempt to separate references to the movie *2012* from references to the year. So they just left that movie out of their analysis. The movies they included seem to span the full range of critical and box office success: from *Avatar* and *The Blind Side* at one end of the scale to *Did You Hear About the Morgans?* and *Transylmania* at the other end.

The first level of analysis they applied was simply to consider the rate of tweets per hour that referred to a given movie. All the tweet had to do was mention the movie. The tweet rate by itself had a respectable correlation to box office receipts ($R = 0.89$ or $R^2 = 0.8$). They could improve the model even further by including how the tweet rate changed over time ($R^2 = 0.93$) and the number of theaters the film opened in ($R^2 = 0.97$). Their model was significantly better than a news media–based model relying on experts and critical reviews. It is remarkable that a model that captures nothing about the actual meaning of the tweet could predict movies so well. (See Exhibit 7.1)

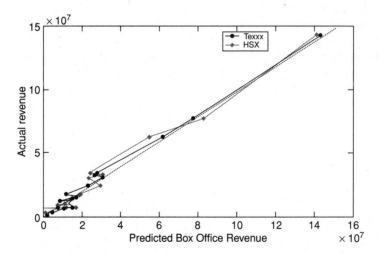

EXHIBIT 7.1   Chart from Huberman and Asur's Research Correlating Tweets to Movie Box Office Receipts

Source: Bernardo Huberman and Sitaram Asur, "Predicting the Future with Social Media," HP Labs, 2010.

Huberman and Asur wanted to go further than just the tweet count. They wanted to gauge the *sentiment* each tweet conveyed about a movie and determine if that could improve the predictive power of the model. There was already a well-developed body of work about measuring sentiment form text, available at least since 2004.[2] In fact, sentiment analysis had been applied to predicting box office success in 2006, based on research using a much smaller sample of the traditional blogs, not Twitter, which had just launched that year.[3] (Huberman and Asur did not cite this work, although they did cite work in the broader field of sentiment analysis.) Never before was there an opportunity to apply sentiment analysis to such a large body of data as there now was with Twitter. Still, improving on the previous model would be difficult if only because the researchers had already reached such high correlations. In other words, there wasn't much room to improve.

Following a protocol developed five years earlier for analyzing blog opinions, each tweet would be classified as having positive, neutral, or negative sentiment. To do this, Huberman and Asur took a sample of their tweets to "train" a linguistic analysis tool called LingPipe. They selected samples of tweets and prepared them for an objective review by human readers. Codes like User IDs, URLs, and most special characters were removed, and the name of the movie was replaced with the text <MOV>. In other words, all the human judge would see was something like "I think <MOV> sounds like a great movie."

To get enough judges to evaluate the thousands of samples they needed to train the linguistic analysis tool, they used a ready army of very inexpensive workers from Amazon Mechanical Turk. (See "Amazon Mechanical Turk—Artificial Artificial Intelligence.") A worker was asked to evaluate each tweet as positive, negative, or neutral about the film. The linguistic analysis software would then attempt to find words and phrases that correlated well with the votes the tweets would get. For example, words like "fantastic" or "great" might correlate with positive votes while "boring" or "lame" might correlate with negative votes. The software also had enough sense to change the sentiment if a word was preceded by "not," as in "not good" or "not bad."

Once Huberman and Asur had trained the linguistic analysis tool, they applied it to the entire set of tweets and determined whether each tweet was positive, negative, or neutral about the movie it mentioned. From this, they computed what they termed the subjectivity and the polarity of a movie. The subjectivity would be equal to the total of all negative and positive tweets divided by neutral tweets. The polarity would be measured with the "PN ratio," or the ratio of positive to negative tweets. When they included this information in the models, they saw only a negligible improvement over the model that simply counted tweets that mention a movie.

Amazon Mechanical Turk—Artificial Artificial Intelligence

Sometimes assessing the Pulse means making thousands of judgments about things like "Is this a positive movie review?" or "What image is in this photograph?" You could use artificial intelligence (AI), but if you don't want to wait for HAL 9000 to finally appear, you can use artificial artificial intelligence (AAI). This was the secret behind an amazing eighteenth-century robot that could play chess very well over 200 years before IBM's Deep Blue. The "Turk" was a mechanical device that looked like a man dressed in Turkish attire sitting at a large table with a chess board before him. The Turk astounded the aristocrats who played against it, but it was, in fact, an illusion. Under the table was a master chess player who operated the arms of the chess-playing robot.

Amazon has re-created a version of this in Amazon Mechanical Turk, a service that allows a "requester" to post a large number of tasks that would be very difficult for a computer but are easy for humans. Each Human Intelligence Task (HIT) could be tagging a single photo or rating the sentiment of a single tweet. Turk workers (aka Turkers) see the HIT posted and are paid on a first-come, first-serve basis.

The first thing I did with Amazon Mechanical Turk was to pay Turkers to fill out a survey about Turk Work. I surveyed 200 people (at 10 cents each, this survey cost me $20), and it was completed in less than a day. About 40% of the respondents were from the United States, 40% were from India, and the rest were distributed around the world. Of these Turkers, 41% said Turk Work comprises all or most of their income. (Some who do it for just part of their income admit doing it while at their full-time job.) Turkers complete each HIT for a price that is usually less than 10 cents and very rarely more than a dollar. HITs are often very quick tasks, such as checking a single link on a web page, but a single requester can post a job with thousands of HITs. Since each HIT often only requires a few seconds to perform, Turkers generally can earn at least a few dollars an hour doing work at their own pace and on their own schedule.

Amazon Mechanical Turk has been useful in multiple studies involving the analysis of text including the research by Huberman and Asur to predict box office receipts and by Alan Mislove to track the national mood (See "Pulse of the Nation"). Since real AI has some catching up to do before it can be of much use assessing the Pulse, a tool like AAI can fill in the gaps until something better comes along.

Of course, it was hard to beat a model that already had an R^2 of .97 (the theoretical maximum being 1). But in other areas, Huberman and Asur discovered that sentiment made all the difference in predicting the future. By the time they got their research published, another group of researchers at Carnegie Mellon University had been measuring tweet sentiment for two years. Huberman and Asur cite some of this earlier research and, in fact, HP funded some of it. This time, however, the sentiment being measured would not be about movies but about the entire economy.

Predicting the Broader Economy with Tweets

In 2009, two professors and two students at Carnegie Mellon University (CMU) in Pittsburgh began using their own sentiment measurement to try to predict a particular measure of the economy: the telephone-based Gallup poll for consumer confidence. In the course of this research, they discovered a kind of threshold in the data in mid-2008. That was when Twitter became a good predictor of economic confidence (and perhaps many other things).

The CMU research began as a class project led by PhD candidates Brendan O'Connor and Ramnath Balasubramanyan. The class was a text-based forecasting seminar being given by Professor Noah Smith. Smith's PhD is in computer science, but one of his undergraduate degrees was in linguistics. His focus has generally been within the area of natural language processing, the problem of getting a computer to understand human language. Smith became interested in predictions about future real-world events and measurements based on a computational analysis of relevant text. Such methods sometimes had been applied to problems like measuring the happiness of song lyrics or measuring the mood of the nation (see the box titled "Pulse of the Nation"), but Smith was interested in forecasting things with measurably verifiable outcomes. This way he could know whether a forecast was right, and the method could be tested scientifically.

Sitting in the class was Bryan Routledge, a finance professor at CMU. Like Smith, Routledge was interested in practical forecasting tools. Routledge and Smith had worked together previously on the analysis of the language of the Form 10-K reports that corporations are required to file annually.[4] There is a lot of quantitative financial data in such reports, and most economic models using the 10-K rely entirely on the numbers. There is also a significant amount of data in text form, including the description of risks, legal proceedings, and management's discussion of the firm's financial strength. Smith and Routledge found that their statistical analysis of the text did predict the volatility of stock prices. They also found that their text-based regression models predicted volatility much better after the Sarbanes-Oxley Act was passed in 2002, an indication of the success of legislation that was meant to improve the quality of financial disclosures.

They designed a methodology similar to what was used in the 2006 research regarding the use of blogs (before Twitter) to predict movie success. The difference was that now they had a lot more data to work with. The CMU team used a list of 2,800 words from OpinionFinder, an open-source opinion analysis toolkit. OpinionFinder rates each word as positive or negative and this information is used to assess the sentiment of text. This lexicon also distinguishes between strong and weak words, but the CMU researchers did not use that information. They simply considered a tweet to be positive if it contained any positive word and negative if it contained any negative word. From this, they could compute a ratio of positive to negative tweets similar to what Huberman and Asur had done.

Smith and Routledge were using the Garden Hose API from Twitter, which gathers a real-time stream of a small percentage of tweets every day. A total of about 1 billion total tweets from early 2008 to the end of 2009 would be collected for the study. The actual sample size varied a lot—from about 100,000 to 7 million tweets per day—partly due to the fact that Twitter grew so fast during the study. By the end of their study in the 2009, Twitter had about 30 million tweets per day. The positive to negative sentiment ratio in tweets that mentioned jobs-related topics was computed every day, and this was compared to the daily Gallup Economic Confidence poll, which is based on a daily survey of 1,000 Americans.

Like Huberman and Asur, they had to apply some commonsense tweaking to tweets. For this study, they looked at words in tweets that might correlate with economic confidence—like "jobs." Routledge noted: "Our metric went a little wonky when the iPhone came out and 'jobs' referred to Steve Jobs." They also saw that you can't just use the word "job" instead of "jobs." If you do, the correlation changes dramatically because, apparently, people use the singular "job" in different contexts than the plural.

At first, their research did not show strong correlations between tweets and Gallup. But by mid-2008, the correlations got much better. (See Exhibit 7.2.) The CMU researchers wondered if the change in the population of tweets over that time could have been the reason for this improved correlation between tweet traffic and traditional polls. This is entirely possible since when their study started, in early 2008, there were less than a million tweets a day. Some kind of threshold was passed in the summer of 2008, and Twitter became large enough, diverse enough, and dynamic enough to predict something useful about the economy.

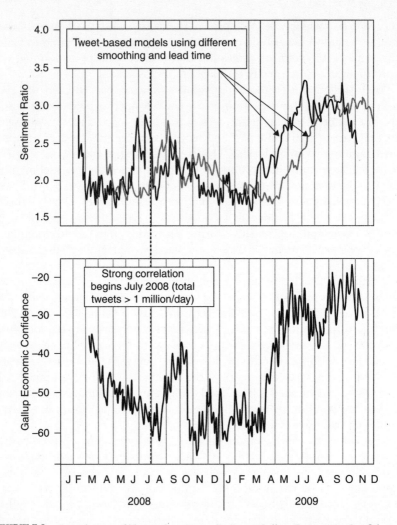

EXHIBIT 7.2 Correlation of Tweet Sentiment Ratio to Gallup Economic Confidence

Source: B. O'Connor, R. Balasubramanyan, B. Routledge, and N. Smith. "From Tweets to Polls: Linking Text Sentiment to Public Opinion Time Series." Proceedings of the International AAAI Conference on Weblogs and Social Media, Washington, DC, May 2010.

They also tried smoothing their model, which involves taking a rolling average over a window of several days. Smoothing helps since volatility in tweets is higher than volatility in the Gallup poll. They also tried different lead times in the model. The lead time difference offsets the tweet data and correlates it to Gallup data from several days later. If one variable predicts the other, then we would see a better correlation with some lead time than without any lead time. The CMU team eventually could predict Gallup up to three weeks in advance.

Their study also considered how well Twitter correlates to presidential approval ratings and the favorability of candidates prior to the 2008 U.S. presidential election. They looked at tweets that mentioned Barack Obama and prior to the election they also looked at tweets that mentioned John McCain. The researchers found that prior to the election, the simple count of tweets that mentioned Obama correlated well to his poll numbers (R = 0.52), but this model improved substantially with smoothing the data over a 15-day window (R = 0.79). The converse was not true for McCain. In fact, increased mentions of McCain seemed to correlate well with *Obama's* poll numbers (R = 0.74).

The authors offer one explanation for this outcome: "A simple explanation may be that frequencies of either term *McCain* or *Obama* are general indicators of elections news and events, and most 2008 elections news and events were favorable toward or good for Obama." There could also be demographic differences between Twitter users. If they tended to be more liberal than a random sample of the entire population, perhaps mentions of McCain would be more likely to be of the negative sort. But even if that were the case, the study supports the idea that Twitter can be used to detect public opinions. The reason is that even this odd outcome or weak correlations are *at least detectable in the data*. The analysis of the Twitter data itself shows where it is strongest and where it is weaker. That is what we need for a good, scientific measurement instrument.

Of course, the real goal with the Pulse is not simply to predict traditional polling methods. They have their own errors, as pointed out in Chapter 2. And as pointed out in Chapter 5 on the use of search behavior to predict trends, the aim of consumer sentiment polls is to *forecast consumer spending*. As we found out in that same chapter, search behavior is a better forecast of spending than traditional polling methods. The real test would be to see how much better tweets predicted actual consumer spending. Routledge recognizes this point and told me: "We did Gallup poll consumer confidence as something to do. But linking it to economic trends would be much more interesting."

Smith, Routledge, and their colleagues see room to improve the sophistication of the text analysis. Routledge admits: "Our analysis is rather coarse. We look at word frequencies and some word pairs." Looking farther down the road, Routledge sees more questions to ask. "A deep question is what language really matters. The thing we do not sort out in our paper is what drives what. How much of Twitter is reflecting activity that happened versus what will happen?" says Routledge; "Noticing that people buy jackets in the fall does not mean that they cause winter." Even so, the tweet sentiment does appear to predict economic confidence even if it doesn't cause it.

Pulse of the Nation

Alan Mislove, an assistant professor at the College of Computer and Information Science, Northeastern University, Boston, has mapped tweet sentiment in the United States by time of day and state. Using over 300 million tweets from 2006 to 2009, he developed what he calls the "Pulse of the Nation." He used Amazon Mechanical Turk (see the earlier box in this chapter) to categorize the moods for a large sample of the tweets and then found words in the text of each tweet that correlated with the moods assigned by Turk Workers. From this he could create a "mood map" of the United States. (See Exhibit 7.3.)

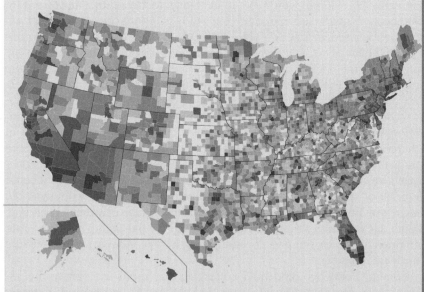

EXHIBIT 7.3   Tweet Volumes across the United States (darker areas are higher volume)

Source: Alan Mislove.

His work received a burst of (traditional) media attention in the summer of 2010 from the CBS Evening News, Fox News, the *New York Times*, *Vanity Fair*, and the *Wall Street Journal* among others. As he tracked tweet sentiment through the entire United States, he observed how the mood changed nationwide throughout both the day and the week. (See Exhibit 7.4.) He also observed that the West Coast is happier than the East Coast. As of this writing, Mislove was still validating his results. He is also who I credit for first using the word *Pulse* in this context. His ultimate hope was to use the Pulse for predictive purposes.

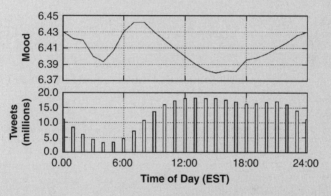

EXHIBIT 7.4   How the National Mood Changes throughout the Day
Source: Alan Mislove.

Predicting Markets with Anxiety

About one and a half centuries before social media came on the scene, Henry David Thoreau stated that most of "the mass of men lead lives of quiet desperation." We still may lead lives as equally desperate as those in Thoreau's time, but today we are not all that quiet about it. And, it turns out, measuring the amount of publicly displayed desperation—or at least the related feeling of anxiety—can be very useful. If you could have measured anxiety on a nationwide scale back in 2008, you might have been able to pick up on the market downturn two or three days before it happened.

One of the researchers looking into the connection between moods and markets is Johan Bollen. He was first mentioned back in Chapter 3 as the researcher who found a correlation between Twitter sentiment and the Dow Jones Industrial Average (DJIA). Whereas the CMU team was basically predicting the output of another survey tool (Gallup), Bollen was predicting a more direct measure of the market. (The DJIA is at least a somewhat more direct and relevant measure if you are invested in the market.)

Bollen is a recent U.S. citizen (a native of Belgium), and prior to becoming an associate professor at Indiana University (IU)–Bloomington, he had worked on similar research at Los Alamos National Laboratory. Although he is in the School of Informatics and Computing at IU, his PhD is in psychology. As this book has shown, his background is consistent with the interdisciplinary nature of a field that also includes computer scientists, linguists, sociologists, epidemiologists, and economists.

Bollen says he likes using Twitter data just because he and other researchers have found "a bunch of really cool results" with the data. He has developed his own way to model several different dimensions of moods on Twitter. He calls his six-variable sentiment tool the Google Profile of Mood States (GPOMS). It is an extension of the Profile of Mood States Bipolar Form, a fairly well-established protocol for measuring moods in text.[5] Like other methods discussed previously, GPOMS organized words into different categories and each word is assigned a value. But unlike the previous methods, it has more categories of words than just negative or positive. The six dimensions of Bollen's model are:

Calm ←→ Anxious
Clearheaded ←→ Confused
Confident ←→ Unsure
Energetic ←→ Tired
Agreeable ←→ Hostile
Elated ←→ Depressed

For comparison, Bollen also used the word list from OpinionFinder (mentioned previously) for positive and negative words. Bollen found that, in this case, the positive and negative terms as labeled by OpinionFinder had no correlation to the DJIA. Nor did he find any strong correlation in five of the dimensions of his GPOMS. He found that the only correlation to market moves was the calm versus anxiety dimension. Furthermore, the best correlation was when he used a lead time of two or three days in the tweets. In other words, his model showed that calmness as measured by tweets about the market predicted fairly well the DJIA two or three days later.

Another study using data from the same period also found a correlation between anxiety and the Standard & Poor (S&P) 500 index with a two-day lead time. Eric Gilbert and Karrie Karahalios of the University of Illinois Urbana-Champaign studied over 20 million posts in the social media site LiveJournal from 2008.[6] LiveJournal is similar to Twitter but allows users who post to tag the post with a "mood" like happy, silly, or even fearful.

This information allowed Gilbert and Karahalios to use a different method for analysis from what has been described in this chapter so far.

Since most of the posts did not have any tagged mood, Gilbert and Karahalios used the same linguistic tool "training" method mentioned earlier to teach linguistic software about which types of words in the text are correlated with which tagged moods. They sampled over 12,000 posts that were tagged as anxious, worried, nervous, or fearful along with thousands of posts that were not tagged this way. Then they used these two sample sets to train their text-analysis software. They used the newly trained, word-spotting software to count words that had been associated with posts that were tagged as anxious. When they compared this to the S&P 500 data, they found a correlation of 0.71 ($R^2 = .51$); the best correlation was when they had a two-day lag between the posts and the market data.

The studies just mentioned are two respectable, peer-reviewed works. We should have some confidence in the idea that mood says something about where the market will be going and that blogs and micro-blogs say something about mood. However, two caveats are needed: First, if you plan on making money on using the findings of these studies to time the market, you are probably too late. Some researchers suspect that some hedge fund managers are already using methods like Bollen's. The arbitrage opportunity may already be gone. Also, both studies were based on 2008 financial data, which was an outlier year for the market, and outliers can change the outcome of a study. As Gilbert and Karahalios stated in their research: "Perhaps in normal times, a pop-culture event like Michael Jackson's death utterly swamps the Anxiety Index. For example, the Anxiety Index has a blip coinciding with Valentine's Day. Maybe in normal times this is a towering event—but not in 2008." Still, all of these studies showed that when people tweet, it is not all random banter. They say something that indicates mood and perhaps intent of future actions. And with sample sizes well into the millions, you can have lots of random noise and still get a strong signal.

Tools and Miscellanea for Tapping into the Global Mood

Most of the recent work on the use of posts in social media to predict major trends has focused on Twitter. The 2006 study on the use of blog posts about movies to predict box office results and the study comparing LiveJournal posts to the S&P 500 were exceptions. Twitter has taken the lead not just because of volume (which is clearly an advantage) but also due to the accessibility of its data. Johan Bollen sums the situation up in this way: "The only reason everyone is talking about Twitter is not because it is a particularly good data set but because they release the data and it is large. Twitter has benefited greatly from this. It fostered an entire industry of Twitter-derived data analysis. They are developing a Twitter ecology."

As we have seen, even random banter does not throw off the ability of resources like blogs and Twitter to find useful signals that predict a practical trend. Still, skepticism exists not only because many posts contain inane or irrelevant banter but because most posts do not merit a response by another person. In the fall of 2010, Sysomos, a business intelligence firm specializing in social media, sampled 1.2 billion tweets and determined that 71% do not get a response of any kind. Somehow, it propagated through the blogosphere and some mainstream media that a survey determined that 71% of tweets are *ignored*—meaning there was no response to the tweet. Sysomos did not use that word in its report. Nor would the usefulness of the data be undermined if tweets were ignored.

Sysomos considered a response to be a "retweet" (a reader of a tweet passing on a tweet as his or her own) or a direct reply to the person who made the original tweet (this is sometimes called an "@reply"). The lack of either response is not evidence that the tweet was not read with interest by someone. What I find interesting is that, apparently, over 29 million tweets each day *do* generate either a retweet or @reply. (I guess I'm a glass-is-29%-full kind of guy).

And regardless of whether another person ever responds to a message, the studies shown so far should be enough to prove that tweets can be useful for forecasting. Our online conversations, no matter how random, inane, or "ignored" our posted thoughts might be, do appear to correlate with—and even predict—trends in measures of the economy and public opinion. These are facts that businesses and governments can and should pay attention to. Here are some things to keep in mind to fully exploit the correlation between our online tweets and real-world trends:

- Tweet volumes will be critical for tracking public opinion on a narrow topic, such as a specific product or brand. Movies seem to generate enough volume to make useful predictions of box office receipts. Major car models or mobile phone models probably also generate useful volumes. But a specific product of a lesser-known brand probably will not generate enough data to predict sales. If you make furniture and want to see how your line of traditional-style living room couches are doing, don't be surprised if your product or even brand doesn't show up in large volumes. There may, however, be sufficient volumes for an entire industry or for large competitors.
- As in search pattern research mentioned in Chapter 5, tweaking the words we search for in social media posts does matter. As the CMU team found, the term "job" is not as useful as "jobs" when searching for words that correlate to opinions about the economy. Developing better lists of words for predicting certain phenomena is a wide-open area of research.

- Don't forget about comments on Facebook, YouTube videos, and customer reviews on Amazon or eBay. Twitter may be a large part of our online conversations, but there is a lot of variety. Most people post product reviews much less often than they tweet or post on their wall on Facebook, but there can still be significant volumes of text to sample, especially because those posts are so purpose-specific.

- Remember to exploit the friend effect discussed in Chapter 6. If you want to gauge the national mood and you have information about social networks as well as daily postings, you might focus on the popular people first. By "popular," I don't mean celebrities; I mean the popular people like those you know personally. Analysis of Facebook wall postings of people who have lots of friends or of tweets of those who have many followers might add even more forecasting range, just as it did with the flu virus.

- The variation in the response rate mentioned in Sysomos report could actually be very useful. The Sysomos survey found that 92% of retweets and 96% of @replies are done in the first hour after the original tweet. The popularity and influence of a tweet will be known very quickly. Most tweets will get only a single reply or retweet, but that is enough to classify some tweets as slightly more representative of an overall buzz on a topic.

- "Social spam" exists, but it does not have to throw off forecasts. It certainly existed during both the CMU and the HP Labs studies. So the mere existence of social spam does not appear to make this research impossible. Still, it may be desirable to filter out some advertising, especially when particular ad volumes reach an unusually large scale. (The advertising would have to be on a gigantic scale to affect the measures in such giant sample sizes.) To help separate the useful sentiments from spam, Johan Bollen launched a site at www.truthy.indiana.edu that analyzes "Truthiness" (a term coined by Stephen Colbert, of the popular faux-news show *The Colbert Report* on the Comedy Channel). The site analyzes sentiments that are really just deliberate viral marketing noise. Bollen calls the noise "social pollution."

Although it is certainly feasible and even economical for a firm to develop its own tracking tools based on screen scrapers and APIs, doing so is not always necessary now. Some of the most powerful software tools and services in this area did not exist prior to 2010. Here are just a few of the more useful tools available:

- Nielsen Buzzmetrics and BlogPulse are tools that analyze blogs and they are available now. Of course, you have to pay for the analysis, but it is a good example of a third-party provider of the Pulse.

- Tools like SAS Social Media Analytics allow an organization to conduct its own analysis of blogs and Twitter. As mentioned in the previous chapter, this is heavy-weight statistical analysis software, and its SMA tool has features for analyzing everything mentioned in the chapter.
- If you had known about some of these promising applications a year or two ago, you could have been harvesting and analyzing blogs and tweets about your firm and already have millions of relevant posts. Fortunately, one firm has been archiving this information for you. Boardreader.com in Toronto is a SAS partner, and it already has over two years of data on blogs on about any topic you want.
- Crimson Hexagon is a third-party provider of Pulse services. It uses its software platform to analyze billions of pieces of information from social media including tweets, Facebook posts, forums, and so forth. You can track opinion on various topics. It has been a provider of social media analysis for CNN.

I've spoken to several researchers who, without any prompting, mentioned how active this field has been just since mid-2009. Conferences are being held and papers are being published even as I write these words. Here are a couple of additional developments worth mentioning:

- Facebook is already exploiting sentiment analysis of texts to wall posts on Facebook. The Gross National Happiness (GNH) mood index is what Facebook proposes as an alternative measure of the economy. Based on the page at http://apps.facebook.com/usa_gnh/, it appears that the GNH is mostly a function of our holidays. According to the GNH, we feel better around Christmas and Thanksgiving (contrary to some measures that say depression increases during the holidays). But even removing the holiday outliers on the chart, it appears we are at least out of the doldrums we had at the end of 2008. Of course, this metric will get a lot more interesting if Facebook can find other measures to validate the GNH against and then find strong correlations.
- Since at least 2005, when there were about a million blog posts each day, intelligence agencies were combing through blogs to gather information on enemy activities. By that time there were 10 million blogs and probably at least a few hundred in regular use by enemies of the United States. Scanning blogs for information isn't really that much different from the "content analysis" done with local newspapers during World War II (see Chapter 2). Fortunately, we no longer need an army of clerks cutting out articles and filing them in manila folders. Furthermore, the total number of local papers worldwide never approached the number of blogs updated every day today.

- Twitter is taking some role in emergency response, and organizations like the Red Cross are trying to improve how they use it.[7] When the earthquake hit Haiti in 2010, many trapped people communicated any way they could, including texting and Twitter. But emergency services did not yet have a good way to respond, and relief workers had to sort through messages manually. And even though organizations like the Red Cross say that 911 is still the best way to contact authorities in an emergency, an online survey conducted by the Red Cross showed that more people say they would use social media in a crisis.[8] Perhaps when people are worried about battery life waiting on hold for swamped dispatchers, sending a text message seems like the best option.

The use of tweets and blogs is one of the more powerful tools of the Pulse and changes in this area will happen fairly rapidly. As with other research topics mentioned in this book, go to www.pulsethenewscience.com for live examples and downloadable content for analyzing the national mood and the Pulse with tweets.

This chapter covered the last among the three areas of the Pulse with the strongest research and the largest amount of publicly available data. What we search for, whom we friend, and what we say are, at this point, the strongest parts of the Pulse. The next chapter looks at some areas where the research is less developed or where the online data is not yet accessible to the general public: our geographic location, what we buy, and what we play online. The research that already exists in the following chapter and the volumes of the data from these mostly unexplored sources will make the Pulse an even more diverse and useful measure of society.

Notes

1. B. Jansen et al. "Twitter Power: Tweets as Electronic Word of Mouth," *Journal of the American Society for Information Science and Technology* (November 2009).
2. M. Hurst and K. Nigam. "Retrieving Topical Sentiments From Online Document Collections," *Proceedings of the 11th Conference on Document Recognition and Retrieva*, 2004.
3. G. Mishne and N. Glance. "Predicting Movie Sales From Blogger Sentiment." Association for the Advancement of Artificial Intelligence (AAAI) 2006 Spring Symposium on Computational Approaches to Analysing Weblogs.
4. K. Shimon, D. Levin, J. Sagi, N. Smith, and B. Routledge. "Predicting Risk from Financial Reports with Regression," *North American Chapter of the Association for Computational Linguistics - Human Language Technologies (NAACL-HLT)*, (June 2009).
5. M. Lorr et al. "A Bipolar Multifactor Conception of Mood States." *Personality and Individual Differences*, 10. no. 2. (1989): 155–159.

6. E. Gilbert and K. Karahalios. "Widespread Worry and the Stock Market." *Proceedings of the Fourth International AAAI Conference on Weblogs and Social Media,* 2010.

7. S. Kinzie. "As People in Distress Turn to Twitter, the Red Cross Seeks the Most Efficient Ways to Respond," *Washington Post,* August 12, 2010.

8. "Social Media in Disasters and Emergencies," American Red Cross report. August 5, 2010.

CHAPTER 8

Three Potential Pulses:
Where We Go, What We Buy,
and How We Play

The data revolution is here for social science. For the first time, scientists have a chance to study what humans do in real-time and in an objective way. It's going to fundamentally change all fields of science that deal with humans.

—Albert Laszlo Barabasi, Northeastern University,
as quoted in *New Scientist*, July 2010

We've seen that online search patterns, social networks, and blogging/ micro-blogging have all been correlated with interesting forecasts about disease outbreaks, political opinions, employment, and even how much money a movie can make. Each of these findings has been held to the standard of scientifically sound tests based on extensive empirical evidence and—with one exception (some parts of the social network research)—the research was based on publicly available data.

But all three of these activities together, according to Nielsen research, still only make up only about 26% of our time online.[1] Other online activities generate a large amount of data and potentially could be valuable parts of the Pulse but currently don't meet our stated requirements. They don't (yet) have solid scientific research showing how they track and predict some real-world trend. Or where good research does exist, it was based on data that was not publicly available on the Internet.

Where we go, what we buy, and how we play are three potential treasure troves of data for the Pulse. Together, these three may account for another 20% of all activities spent online. This 20% doesn't even have to include tracking our physical location since, in principle, that data could be gathered entirely passively. More importantly, the go-buy-play trio is a particularly data-rich set of activities from which we may be able to infer many interesting macro-trends. While rarer in these three areas, the research that does exist and the data that is public is enough for us to connect the dots and see another great source of the Pulse.

Our Flow and the Pulse: What the Movements of Millions of People Tell Us

Marketers, architects, and city planners have long known the value of measuring the flow of people. Counts of the cars in a mall parking lot or people going through a particular airport have been used for measuring retail activity, for estimating migration of populations, and for identifying potential strains on public resources. These methods don't actually track individuals from point to point as they travel. They are not real time nor are the data granular enough that someone could reconstruct social networks from their travels.

But real-time, massive, and passively gathered location data will be a boon to the social sciences. Location sharing is a relatively recent but growing feature of the Internet and social media. According to a Pew Research survey, 4% of all online Americans use some kind of location-based service.[2] As first mentioned in Chapter 3, by early 2010, there were already over 7,000 apps that use GPS (Global Positioning System) locations of mobile phones. Most of these apps are for the iPhone, and 90% of them are free. Location-based services include the use of "geosocial" apps like Foursquare or Gowalla, which allow users to find friends near them. An app named Yelp lets the user write and read location-based reviews of local businesses; it might be possible to count these reviews as indicators of economic activity. Mobile versions of both Facebook and Twitter allow for locations to be included in updates automatically.

When a large number of people share their location, the aggregated data can signal important activities and trends. It tells us the density of people, the rate of movement, whether they are next to shopping or government services, what other people they may be meeting, and more. If location data is combined with text communications and other activities, even more information can be derived. Current research that exists has not been performed with the publicly available data, but the potential has been proven.

In 2005, well before the wide availability of location-based services, one PhD candidate at the Massachusetts Institute of Technology (MIT) Media Labs wrote a dissertation proving how important location data would be in mapping social networks (mentioned briefly in chapter 2). Nathan Eagle, who at the time of this writing is a visiting assistant professor at MIT, found that if we compared what people remembered and *said* about their social lives and where they *actually* went, something didn't match up. His findings would help to overturn and partly replace surveys as the fundamental tool of social research.

In the twentieth century, the kinds of data that were used for social science research were very limited; in some cases studies depended on data from social groups collected several decades before. As early as the 1970s and 1980s, research began to show there was often little correlation between self-reported data about social interaction and actual behavior.[3] Eagle calls this "a phenomenon that many within the social sciences chose to ignore." He recognized the potential for better data sources:

> *The field [of social science] is about to become inundated with massive amounts of data that is not just limited to human behavior in the online world; soon datasets on almost every aspect of human life will become available. And while social scientists have become quite good at working with sparse datasets involving discrete observations and surveys of several dozen subjects over a few months, the field is not prepared to deal with continuous behavioral data from thousands—and soon millions—of people. The old tools simply won't scale.*[4]

Instead of relying on periodic, self-assessment surveys for data on social networks, Eagle conducted a study using one of the early "smartphones" to track the location and communication of his subjects in great detail. He recruited 100 students at MIT and gave them each what was then a top-of-the-line smartphone—the Nokia 6600. Each phone was preloaded with an application that shared locations estimated from cell tower locations.

The phone further refined the location data with a method for continuous scanning of Bluetooth—the short-range device communication protocol used by wireless earpieces. The location-finding methods based on cell phone tower location was too inaccurate to determine if two people were close enough to be socializing, but the short-range Bluetooth scan could easily determine that. Also, the subjects' use of cameras, calendars, and other phone apps was monitored. Subjects were given discretion over disengaging the logging as well as deleting logged data. Subjects participated in this study in exchange for the phone, which was then new and was available only in Finland.

Over a nine-month period, Eagle was able to collect approximately 300,000 hours of detailed behavioral data on the 100 subjects in his study. He also had the subjects fill out several (traditional) surveys about what they believed their social life to be like. With this amount of detailed data,

Eagle could infer general rules of behavior and even compute a probability for the future behavior of a given individual.

A key finding that stood out was the difference between the social encounters people believed they had over a previous week and what could be verified by Bluetooth encounters. While self-reported social encounters of seniors were fairly consistent with their Bluetooth encounters, self-reported social encounters of the freshmen were entirely inconsistent with Bluetooth encounters. Both groups were also highly inaccurate at remembering whom they talked to and for how long. If most previous social science studies depended on self-reported data collected by surveys, and if those surveys are shown to be incompatible with basic facts, such as a person's recorded location history, then most social science studies must be fundamentally flawed.

Eagle's study used cell towers and Bluetooth to determine locations, but mobile phone users generate location data in several ways today. Many phones and even cameras today also have GPS. Since GPS relies on direct triangulation with satellites, it is even more available and sometimes more accurate than cell tower location methods. Location sometimes can be inferred from other communications, such as explicit references in text or photos. Conceivably, even the accelerometers (devices that detect movement by measuring acceleration) which are available in most smartphones could be used in refining location data.

This location data sometimes is embedded into photos or tweets by "geotagging." With image files, location data may be embedded using the "exchangeable image file format" (EXIF). In most digital cameras or smartphones with any GPS capability, posting the geotag on the photo is actually the *default* choice. Many people posting photos online may not know that the location data is part of the photo file format and that this publicly available information could also be mined. Apps on mobile phones may also aggregate this information and report general traffic flow and population density. These apps do not usually make available locations of specific individuals—unless someone opts for it.

In some situations, specific, personal location data is not public but was explicitly and voluntarily reported to some authority. This is called Volunteered Geographic Information (VGI). One situation where people are especially willing to volunteer their own specific locations is when they are in need of help. In a really big crisis where lots of people need help, such as the 2010 earthquake in Haiti, these calls for help formed patterns with other surprising benefits.

Despite the poverty of Haiti, a significant percentage of the population have mobile phones with the ability to send Short Message Service (SMS) text. Recall from Chapter 7 that SMS is the basic protocol utilized by Twitter for text messages of up to 140 characters. The majority of even the most inexpensive mobile phones now have this feature for person-to-person tex-ting. In the days after the January 12, 2010, earthquake, people in heavily damaged areas often resorted to SMS messaging to call for help. This was possible because four days after the earthquake, a system called "Ushahidi" was in place to collect help messages via mobile phones.

Ushahidi is a free and open-source software platform for mapping location-based information from SMS, a smartphone photo, or data submit-ted directly into online sources. Ushahidi, the Swahili word for "witness," has been used for real-time mapping of postelection violence in Kenya, civil unrest in the Democratic Republic of the Congo, and violence in Lebanon. It was also used for monitoring of the 2009 elections in India and world-wide H1N1 flu outbreaks. In Haiti, people in each area of the city were told via radio stations and other channels to spread the word that texting 4636 sends a help message to emergency responders via Ushahidi. People who were able could then text for help on behalf of people who couldn't. Re-searchers at the European Commission Joint Research Center (JRC) subse-quently analyzed this data for a novel application: They wanted to see if they could map the earthquake damage simply by reviewing people's calls for help and where they were when they called.

The JRC researchers fed the SMS data into a model that would pre-dict the intensity of damage based on patterns of the locations where the messages originated. These results were then compared to a much more time-consuming estimation method based on detailed inspections of high-resolution aerial photos. When Christina Corbane, a JRC expert in remote sensing and image processing, compared the two data sets, the fit was strik-ing. "When we saw the data side by side on a computer screen, we could see that something was going on there," says Corbane. I created Exhibit 8.1 using the JRC data as a source, and with some map data for the area as a reference. The darkest areas on the charts are the most damaged areas.

The similarity of these maps is obvious. The map based on detailed expert estimates was more accurate, but creating it also took a significantly longer and more intensive effort. *It took 600 experts from 23 countries over a month to complete inspections of aerial photos of buildings, while the data aggregated on Ushahidi was real time.* In emergencies, approximate infor-mation available now can be much more useful than precise information a lot later.

The work of Corbane and her colleagues was presented at a crisis-mapping conference held in Ispra, Italy in October 2010. In this conference, VGI-based methods were also presented as a way to track such things as forest fires and damage from the 7.1 Richter scale earthquake in Yushu, China. The stated goal of the event was "to explore new avenues in the validation of geo-spatial information derived from Web-based open source data, crowd-sourcing and earth-observation data in the context of crisis

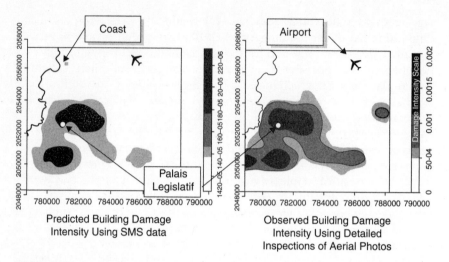

Predicted Building Damage
Intensity Using SMS data

Observed Building Damage
Intensity Using Detailed
Inspections of Aerial Photos

EXHIBIT 8.1   Predicted versus Observed Building Damage in Port-au-Prince, Haiti, after the 2010 Earthquake

Source: C. Corbane et al., "Can Real-Time Crisis SMS Messages Help in Diagnosing the Spatial Distribution of Structural Damage?" Second International Workshop on Validation of Geo-Information Products for Crisis Management, Ispra, Italy, 2010, p. 116, Figures 7a and 7b.

management." This kind of validation is required for acceptance in the scientific and emergency management communities. "We had to see how to build trust about this as an information source," Corbane explains. Results like those from the SMS data gathering after the Haiti earthquake should at least cause any rational scientist to sit up and take notice.

Corbane's work is another example in the history of science and engineering where the availability of the tools drive innovation even though, at first, how the tools would be used was not known. Corbane saw this research as being driven simply by the availability of massive amounts of data. "This topic came out by chance," she notes. "It was not really my main interest to work on this. But it was in the pile of data we had." This fact should remind us that, with the Internet and mobile communications, there are still far more and far larger "piles" of data to explore and much greater potential for discovery.

Some researchers have used location data to map the kinds of social networks Christakis and Fowler (see Chapter 6) used for their research about how health-related measures spread through a network. Anmol Madan, for his PhD dissertation at MIT, showed how the same kinds of social networks could be inferred from Bluetooth scanning and that political opinions and body mass index can be predicted from this information.[5] Madan and other colleagues were also able to show that location data combined with communications could be used to determine the likelihood that someone is ill. When we don't feel well, we change how often we communicate with others and how we move.[6] The authors of this research refer to the field as "spatial and behavioral epidemiology." Their work opens the possibility of crisis management in an epidemic, even if users are unaware of their illness or unable to respond.

As location data becomes more pervasive and more accurate, even more kinds of research will be possible. As of 2010, only about 0.6% of all tweets were geotagged,[7] but that still adds up to over 600,000 geotagged tweets every day, and it leaves plenty of room for growth. As more location-based apps are developed, the incentive for volunteering your location will only increase. Furthermore, the accuracy of location data even without GPS will have to be held to minimum standards as a matter of law. The Federal Communications Commission has established "E911" rules that require, among other things, that any call sent to 911 will also have to provide longitude and latitude data accurate to "within 50 to 300 meters depending on the type of technology used."[8] Of course, this data will be sent directly to emergency responders and will not be available for public consumption. But the fact that the phones must have this capability will inevitably be exploited for other purposes.

The Shopping Pulse

eBay was the first social networking site.
—Meg Whitman, former eBay chief executive officer

Where we actually spend our money can be much more enlightening than how we answer polls. The former is called *revealed* preference and the later a *stated* preference. When a polling organization like Gallup or Pew asks people in a survey if they prefer environmentally friendly products that cost 20% more than other products, the responses are simply what was stated by the persons being surveyed. But if we watch what they actually purchase, that would be an indication of a revealed preference.

As first mentioned in Chapter 3, 71% of Internet users have made an online purchase, and online shopping makes up about 8% of all retail business in the United States at the end of 2010. According to Nielsen Online, only about 2.7% of time spent online is spent shopping. But since purchases are revealed preferences, this 2.7% can tell us a lot.

eBay, one of the largest online retailers, leaves a lot of data for everyone to see. Tens of millions of individual items are available for sale at any moment, and over 200 million items were sold in 2009. Compared to other retailers, its revenues of $8.7 billion in 2009 make it appear to be a much smaller market than it is. Unlike Wal-Mart or Target, eBay only counts its fees as the revenue, not the entire sale, so to compare these retailers, we need to look at total transactions. Total annual transactions for eBay exceeded $60 billion by 2009, which still makes it smaller than the largest retailer (Wal-Mart, $305 billion) but makes it as big or bigger than any retailer in the next tier, such as Target, Home Depot, or Sears. In fact, the number of transactions each day for eBay exceeds the total number on the New York Stock Exchange and Nasdaq combined.

Each auction on eBay has to be publicly visible, just so customers can make bids. But even completed auctions are available for some period of time. Thus, this data could be gathered by scrapers, but just about anything you can see online is also available in free eBay Application Program Interfaces (APIs). The eBay APIs allow developers to comb through prices, item categories, condition (new or used), location, how long the item was for sale, and other bids offered by other buyers. Still, you may not have to use an API to gather such information. Third-party services have been gathering eBay data with the eBay APIs and generating reports for their subscribers for many years. Terapeak, the largest firm specializing solely in eBay research, has been in business since 2002. It can provide its customers detailed historical data by seller and category as well as international eBay research.

And while eBay is just one company, it is not really *one* retailer. There are over 80 million individual sellers on eBay. Unlike Target or Wal-Mart, there is no central price setting—it is a free and fluid market. This kind of detailed data for such a large number of sales available in real time must tell us something about the direction of the entire economy. It should indicate something about nationwide consumer spending and perhaps even inflation. Given that it operates in 190 markets using 23 currencies, it should indicate something about the balance of trade and track (if not predict) exchange rates. The sales of specific categories—such as the over 3,000 items in real estate or the over 3 million in the business and industrial category—should indicate something about the economic trends in specific segments.

Unfortunately, no such research exists, at least at the time this book was written. Nothing like the kind of thorough academic studies done with Twitter or Google Trends—where correlations to government reports or Gallup polls were computed—has been done with this massive and real-time feed of eBay data. The research provided by firms like Terapeak is generally for individual sellers trying to find the best sales strategies (i.e., whether to have a minimum bid, a "buy it now" option, whether to pay to make an item a "featured" product, etc.). It has not been applied to tracking and forecasting general macro-trends in the economy. In fact, eBay might be the most underutilized source of data for the Pulse.

Other kinds of online shopping data also could be used for measuring the Pulse. One purchase that might be informative about trends in society are the books people buy. The purchase of a book, since it costs money, is a bit closer to a revealed preference. People who buy books on, say, home purchases may still not follow through with a home purchase, but buying the book is perhaps a step up from just Googling it.

Although Amazon, the world's largest bookseller, does not post each sale, as eBay does, it does post the Amazon Sales Rank for each book. This rank shows how well the book's sales compare to the other few million books sold on Amazon so that, as I write this, George W. Bush's *Decision Points* is number one in sales and the book *Collecting More Household Linens* ranks about 2 millionth in sales. The ranks are updated at least once per day for books in the top 100,000 or so and hourly for those closer to the top 10,000.

Amazon is secretive about its algorithm for computing sales ranks and warns that they should not be used as a consistent and reliable estimator of sales. But we can use this data if we are careful to validate any conclusions we might draw. By comparing the month-by-month sales of my two previous books to their Amazon Sales Rank, I can make an order-of-magnitude approximation for what the book sales are at a given rank. I also found some online sources that are more or less consistent with what my own data shows.

A rank of 10,000 indicates that about 15 to 25 books are sold per month on Amazon—which means about 80 to 160 books per month total sales from all retailers, including Amazon. (The variation on total books sold is partly due to the fact that Amazon accounts for different percentages of total sales in different genres.) For books ranking between 1,000 and 1,000,000, a good approximation of relative sales is that a rank 10 times smaller means sales of about 6.3 times higher. In other words, a book with a sales rank of about 1,000 sells approximately 6.3 times as much as a book with a rank of 10,000. According to a historical analysis of my own book sales, converting sales rank into monthly book sales can be approximated by the formula:

$$\text{Approximate Amazon Monthly Sales} = 10^{(4.5 - X * 0.8)}$$

where

$$X = \text{the monthly average of the log of the sales rank}$$

This finding mostly agrees with other sources. My books have usually sold with ranks between 1,000 and 40,000, so I cannot directly validate the formula outside of that range. But, according to other sources, this rule seems to work until the ranks are better than about 1,000 or worse than about 1 million. Some sources propose several estimates outside of this range, but none actually discloses the details of how it computes the estimate. The general consensus seems to be that when a book rank gets to be in the hundreds of thousands, sales of an individual book are several days apart, and each sale can be seen as a sudden jump in the book's Amazon book rank. MetricJunkie uses a sales estimating method that actually counts these jumps—which it calls "Cha Chingers"—but with better-selling books, these jumps do not represent an individual sale. The longer a book goes since its last sale, the worse the rank gets, and if a book doesn't sell a copy in a year, its rank slips to 2 million or worse.

Now, let's put this information to use. Suppose we have a predictive model based on books in the "getting out of debt" genre. Perhaps we believe that tracking such books will tell us something about changes in consumer debt. This is only a hypothesis at this point, of course. In order to verify a correlation, we would have to compare the sales of a large number of books in this category to real-world data tracked over a period of at least a couple of years. I don't have two years of data, but, using MetricJunkie, I tracked 19 books in this category from March to the end of November 2010. All of them had ranks from 2,000 to just under 1 million.

I then used my approximation formula to estimate actual sales from book ranks. Since some of the books sold considerably more than others, simply adding up total sales would have mostly reflected the fluctuations in sales of a single book. I decided just to average—for each book—sales relative to sales at the beginning of March. (Each book starts out at 100%, and the percentages, not actual sales, are averaged.) Exhibit 8.2a shows the Amazon sales ranks for a single book in this category, and Exhibit 8.2b shows the relative change of sales compared to the revised monthly data for consumer credit as reported by the U.S. Federal Reserve Bank (FRB). On the Web site www.pulsethenewscience.com, I show a spreadsheet for this calculation as well as the data for how I came up with the estimation formula.

I offset the data from the FRB by shifting if forward four weeks. The Amazon Book index is actually measuring a period four weeks after the

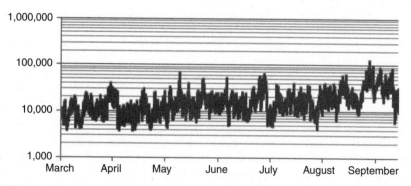

EXHBIBIT 8.2a Amazon Book Rank for a Single Book of the "Getting Out of Debt" Genre, March to September 2010

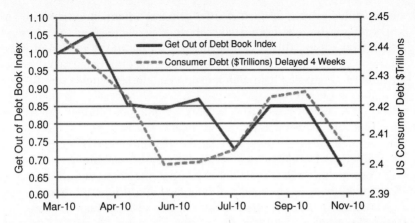

EXHBIBIT 8.2b "Getting Out of Debt" Genre Book Index vs Consumer Debt with time offset, March to September 2010

FRB data shown. However, the book index is still *available a week before the FRB data is reported*. So the book index may be a delayed measure, but it is still not as delayed as the FRB report.

I don't have nearly enough data to validate this finding, but it indicates an interesting possibility. I'll continue to collect this data and post it on www.pulsethenewscience along with a comparison to the FRB consumer debt data. This model could certainly be improved and either validated or disproven by adding a much larger number of books and tracking them for a longer period of time. The sales of individual books fluctuate widely and for reasons that may have more to do with Amazon promotion campaigns than more fundamental changes in the public's reading interests. Different lag times in the data might be used to see if the correlation improves when we use books sales as a predictive model. (See the use of lag and lead times in Chapter 7.)

My "Amazon Index of Economic Trends" clearly needs more work. (After all, I spent only a couple of hours on the analysis.) But an analysis of book sales and the detailed price data of eBay is probably entirely underutilized. There is so much information about what we buy or intend to buy on the Internet that using it to beat traditional government reports should be the focus of at least several dissertations. Whether you are in government, business, or academia, here are a few other items that you might exploit for the part of the Pulse which reveals what we buy:

- Using apps like Google Goggles [9] (by January of 2011, still only available on the Google Labs site) and RedLaser, mobile phones can now scan bar codes or use a photo of a logo to bring up product information, including sales ranks of products, reviews, other sellers, and competitive pricing information. To generate information like competitive prices, the data from each scan must be aggregated and reported back to the user. This is like having a crowd-sourced version of price surveys conducted by the U.S. Department of Commerce. The combination of purchasing data with location data in real time is sure to be a boon to the Pulse.

- One unpublished paper from a Harvard graduate student shows that the ratio of jobs wanted to jobs available classifieds on Craigslist is an indicator of unemployment and that foreclosures could be inferred from classified ads for real estate.[10] Craigslist posts 80 million new classified ads per month, which makes it the largest and most dynamic display of classified ads in any medium, online or not. If research like this can be confirmed, then the analysis of Craigslist ads could open up another area of the Pulse.

- Traffic to a large number of major retail sites as reported by Alexa.com could tell us something about retail spending in the economy. Using not only the number of visitors but also the time spent on the site might improve the forecast. It is conceivable that someone could assemble Alexa data for hundreds or thousands of business Web sites in several different industries and track it real time against industry data. It seems very likely that traffic volumes by industry segment could be informative.

- The number of product reviews, good or bad, could tell us something about the relative popularity of categories of items. Generally, books on Amazon with lots of reviews also sell well. Reviews may be another indirect approximation of sales for sites that don't offer sales ranks.

- Amazon reports sales ranks for all of its nonbook categories, including electronics, home and garden, jewelry, and so on. It is possible that changes in relative sales of luxury versus economy items could track with economic trends.

Playtime and the Pulse

There are over 100 million gamers globally who spend more than an hour a day playing games. That is an extraordinary concentration of time, attention and emotional engagement.
    —Jane McGonigal, *New Scientist*, May 22, 2010

How we spend our time on the Internet enjoying ourselves helps to nowcast and forecast in ways both subtle and direct. Online gaming is definitely the most nascent area of the Pulse, however because we spend so much time in this activity, developing ways to exploit this data could be very useful. Nielsen estimates gaming accounts for 10% of all time spent online, making it second only to social networks as the most time-consuming online activity. Conservatively speaking, this means that there are over 10 million people online playing games *at any given moment*, worldwide, for a total of over 1.6 billion hours of game-play each week. Of course, game time is generated mostly by people under the age of 33 (they account for 67% of all online hours), but 8.5% of all game-play is generated by people 55 and older.

Some hugely popular games are massive multiplayer online games that allow hundreds of thousands of players to engage simultaneously. Games like World of Warcraft (WoW) are both competitive and collaborative, and they may involve playing a single character in a game (role-playing) or grand-scale strategy games. Facebook uses social network–based distribution and game-play for widely popular games like Farmville and Mafia Wars.

Game-play may seem like an even more indirect measure of moods, preferences, and intentions than Twitter or Google searches, but everything in our lives affects everything else in our lives. Research shows that moods do affect play; therefore, observing play can lead to inferences about mood and other elements of people's lives. For example, studies have shown that a person's tolerance for risk can be affected by environmental factors or moods. In one such study, some subjects were instructed to describe past events in their lives that involved fear while other subjects were asked to describe events when they were angry. The "anger" group was found to be more likely to make risky choices than the "fear" group.[11] A small study presented at the Cognitive Neuroscience Society meeting in 2009 showed that simply being briefly exposed to smiling faces makes people more risk tolerant in betting games.[12]

The connection among mood, environment, and choices in games indicates the possibility that massive amounts of game-play data would say something about bigger trends outside of the game. Some data is publicly available for WoW via a site called "The Armory" and a WoW API, but the massive retrieval of detailed data is deliberately made difficult. (Players could use this to manipulate the game.) Some research shows that WoW game data does correlate with basic personality measures, but, to date, no research shows a correlation of the behaviors of millions of players to real-world trends.[13] This is a wide open and potentially very fruitful area of research for the Pulse.

In both of my previous books, I mentioned how one particular type of game has already been shown to be an excellent way to estimate the probabilities of future events. Prediction markets are games where players buy and sell "coupons" that will be worth something—perhaps $1—if some predicted event comes true and worth nothing if it does not come true. The market price of the coupons turn out to be a good approximation of the event's probability.

For example, you might believe your favorite candidate will win the election for governor of your state. In the prediction market, coupons are being traded that will be worth $1 if this particular candidate is elected and worth nothing if the candidate is not elected. You see that the coupons for this prediction are currently selling at only 20 cents. Since you believe that it is very likely this candidate will win, in which case the coupon will be worth $1, you think this coupon is an excellent bargain, so you purchase 100 of them. Other players disagree and are selling them.

Markets like this currently exist for predictions in technology, entertainment, sports, and more. Ideosphere.com is a play-money site that allows you to sign up for free and gives you a weekly allowance of play money to bet with. Other sites like www.intrade.com require players to bet with real money—but some research shows that both play-money and real-money sites are about equally effective in predicting the outcomes of future events. When we look at all events that pay $1 if they come true but currently are priced between 20 and 30 cents, we will find that about 20% to 30% of them eventually came true and paid the holder $1. Of the coupons selling at 80 to 90 cents, about 80% to 90% will eventually come true, and so on.

Exhibit 8.3 shows how closely the market prices of these coupons correlate to the probability that the event eventually came true. The data comes

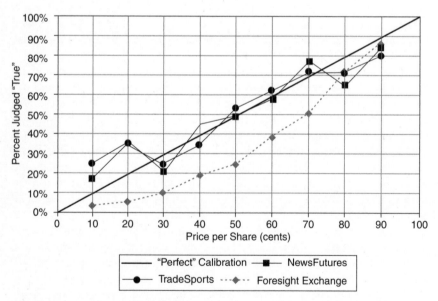

EXHIBIT 8.3 Predicted Odds of an Event (Based on Share Price of Prediction Coupons) and Actual Outcomes

from research comparing Intrade to another service, NewsFutures.com,[14] combined with my own research based on data from ideosphere.com. The Intrade and NewsFutures data shows market prices versus outcomes for National Football League games. On NewsFutures.com, participants did not play with real money but did compete for prizes. The Ideosphere data is from 400 predictions covering a wide range of topics outside of purely sports. The Intrade and NewsFutures data shows very little difference in the two games' ability to assign odds. In both cases, a team won just about as often as the market price predicts. In the case of Ideosphere, the market generally seems to overprice events. The Ideosphere outcomes might be the effect of the players having no monetary consequences, but what is interesting is how *consistently* overpriced the coupons are. With these results as a kind of calibration, a realistic probability of the event still can be estimated from Ideosphere market data.

Other specialized prediction markets have confirmed track records of performance. Since 1998, the University of Iowa has been running the Iowa Electronic Market, a prediction market specializing in political elections. This market outperforms Gallup polls at predicting the outcomes of elections.[15] A market called the Hollywood Stock Exchange has been predicting box office receipts and Academy Awards of movies since and similar markets have even been applied to the likelihood of specific scientific discoveries.[16]

Prediction markets are definitely a much smaller, more niche set of users than other online games. In some markets, the small number of players means that trades are infrequent, and market prices may not really reflect current information in the market. Some research shows that prediction markets are only marginally better than models based on historical data, if such data is available. (If such data were available, it may not be public or dynamically updated.)

However, unlike other online games, prediction markets already have a large amount of publicly available data that can be used to track real-world events and a lot of research to show that they work. And prediction markets have the advantage of being applicable to just about any specific event in any topic, *if* there are enough traders. In fact, prediction markets are the one item in this chapter that already meets all of the requirements for the Pulse: publicly available data and sound research showing it is a reliable measure.

So far, we have discussed how we can use what we search for on the Internet, whom we connect with in social networks, and what we say on the Internet as indicators of major trends. We have also explored less developed or less publicly available data (but equally promising) recording where we go, how we shop, and how we play as possible indicators of threats and opportunities. Next we look at how all this research and all these sources of data impact the decision maker in business or government in practical ways. In the final chapter, we will look at where the Pulse might take us from here.

Notes

1. I added the social networks and search categories from Nielsen NetView. Twitter is categorized as a social network. June 2009/June 2010.
2. K. Zickuhr and A. Smith. "4% of Online Americans Use Location-Based Services," Pew Research Center's Internet & American Life Project. November 4, 2010.
3. H.R. Bernard and P.D. Killworth. "Informant Accuracy in Social Network Data II," *Human Communications Research* 4 (1977): 3–18. H. R. Bernard, P. D. Killworth, D. Kronenfeld, and L. Sailer. "The Problem of Informant Accuracy: The Validity of Retrospective Data," *Annual Review of Anthropology* 13 (1985): 495–517.
4. Eagle, N. *Machine Perception and Learning of Complex Social Systems,* PhD diss., Department of Media Arts and Sciences, MIT, May 2005.
5. A. Madan. *Social Evolution: Opinions and Behaviors in Face-to-Face Networks*, PhD diss., Department of Media Arts and Sciences, MIT, submitted September 2010.
6. A. Madan, M. Cebrian, D. Lazer, and A. Pentland. "Social Sensing for Epidemiological Behavior Change," UbiComp '10, September 26–29, 2010.
7. T. Crampton. "Asia Accounts for 37% of World's Tweets," *Thomas Crampton, Social Media in China and across Asia,* Sept 23, 2010.
8. Federal Communications Commission. "FCC WIRELESS 911 REQUIREMENTS." Federal Communications Commission. N.p., 1 Dec. 2000. Web. 30 Jan. 2011
9. E. Zeman. "Google Goggles Now Recognizes More Languages and Images," *Information Week,* May 6, 2010; accessed online.
10. Z. Aljarboua. "Craigslist & The Economy: Predicting Unemployment and Foreclosure Trends from Online Classified Advertisements," submitted for publication in *Proceedings of the International Conference on Business, Economics, Finance and Management Sciences*, Paris, France, 2010.
11. J. Lerner and D. Keltner. "Fear, Anger and Risk," *Journal of Personality and Social Psychology* (2001).
12. "J. Hall. Cheery Traders May Encourage Risk Taking," *New Scientist*, April 7, 2009.
13. N. Yee et. al. "Introverted Elves & Conscientious Gnomes: The Expression of Personality in World of Warcraft" presented at *CHI 2011*, May 7–12, 2011, Vancouver, BC, Canada.
14. E. Servan-Schreiber et. al. "Does Money Matter?" *Electronic Markets.* Vol. 14, no. 3, (September 2004).
15. P. Gomme, "Iowa Electronic Markets," Economic Commentary, Federal Research Branch of Cleveland. April 15, 2003.
16. D.M. Pennock, S. Lawrence, C.L. Giles, and F.A. Nielsen. "The Real Power of Artificial Markets," *Science* 291, no. 5506. January 2001: 987–988.

PART III

Effects of the Pulse

CHAPTER 9

Making the Pulse Practical

You may delay, but time will not.

—Benjamin Franklin

So far, this book has focused on scientific research—based on mostly publicly available data—that has shown that the Pulse tracks or forecasts big trends. We also reviewed what may be done with the Pulse with a little more scientific research or if the existing data were made publicly available in some form.

Now we turn to how to make the potential of this resource useful for managers. Most businesses have not exploited on a large scale the research on using Twitter for forecasts of movie box office receipts, consumer confidence, or the Dow Jones Industrial Average. Nor have most organizations adopted deliberate campaigns to leverage the research with Google Trends or Facebook to assess changes in demand of a product or the effectiveness of an advertising campaign. We have to address the reasons for this under-utilization of a powerful tool and give some guidance for using the Pulse to its potential in business.

In this chapter, we look at what an organization might do to use real-time information like the Pulse effectively. We need to introduce some basic ideas about the value of information and how it applies to real-time data. We also need to review some potential cultural obstacles to adopting the kinds of methods necessary for the Pulse. Finally, we then look at how the organization can make these recommendations actionable.

Rethinking Real-Time Decisions in the Pulse

The Pulse is a tool unlike any that managers are used to. If managers want to make full use of the Pulse, they will have to reconsider how they make some decisions. As a tool for tracking and forecasting macro-trends, only the Pulse has all three of these features:

1. *The Pulse is real time or very nearly real time yet massive.* Many outward-looking measures exist in the form of government monthly economic figures or periodic customer surveys, but these measures are infrequent, and often the results are available long after the period of time being studied has passed. Most government reports tell us how well some measure of the economy was doing a month ago. Then, the report often is revised so that final data is not available for months. The closest that traditional survey methods get to being real-time are certain polls that are conducted daily with a survey of hundreds of people. Few businesses have such resources available, and even if a business could conduct polls on such a vast scale the results still may not be as accurate and cannot be nearly as massive as the Pulse.

2. *The Pulse is outward looking.* Businesses need to focus on data about customers, competitors, threats, and opportunities outside of or even *before* the traditionally recorded interactions with the company (i.e., a transaction, a security breach, etc.). This is not just a more in-depth look at existing databases of data about orders, inventories, staff, projects, and so on. No matter how large your firm may be, the Internet is a much larger database.

3. *The Pulse is not restricted to data about markets, such as actively traded securities, currencies, or commodities.* Actively traded markets are crowd-sourced streams of information that are real time and are generated by the world outside of a single business. But these are at best highly indirect measures (if any measure at all) of things like public opinion, fads, changing demographics, public health, or security threats.

Managers are used to dealing with up to two of these features at a time, not all three. As I just mentioned, financial markets meet the first two criteria but not the third. Data about manufacturing operations, however, meets the first and third criteria but not the second—it is real-time data that is not just about financial markets, but the data is entirely inward-looking as opposed to being a measure of the outside world. Managers are also used to using large surveys of customers, which includes nonfinancial market data and it is outward-looking but does not have the first feature of being real time while being based on massive data sources.

In combination, all three of these features of the Pulse create a tool that managers must learn to use. Perhaps the biggest challenge is how to exploit real-time data used for measuring something of interest to the business. Even in situations where real-time data is already available (financial markets or purely internal data), dynamically changing measurements based on this data are not always fully leveraged. If managers track and report real-time measurements in some form, they approach using the data in two very different ways:

1. *Exploratory measurements.* With the exploratory measurement approach, you don't know what you might find or what you would do if you found it. You just track data because the measurements simply seem interesting and important. The hope is that if the measurements were surprising in some way, further investigation and analysis would lead to some kind of action. This method can be very useful for purely academic research, but even then only for initial discovery (after which specific research goals and hypotheses are proposed). However, in a business setting, this method probably is acceptable only when the cost of waiting on a decision is negligible, the consequences of a poor decision are low, or no specific decision scenarios or actions can even be imagined. It is highly unlikely that these conditions—especially the condition that no actions can even be imagined—exist for most important business decisions.

2. *Decision-focused measurements.* Ideally, measurements are made with specific decision alternatives defined in advance. Scenarios of various outcomes of measurements are imagined, and deliberate analysis is applied to work out optimal actions in advance. This allows the manager to identify specific, measurable conditions which would merit a particular action. This set of "trigger conditions" based on these measurements are computed for each possible alternative action. The measurements are being tracked specifically to see if and when certain trigger conditions arise. If they do, the predefined action can begin immediately without the delay of further analysis. A human manager still could be the fail-safe protection against an obviously erroneous action. But if that manager were involved in sound decision modeling in the first place, erroneous action would occur less often.

The manager may already be used to some applications of decision-focused measurements. In actively traded markets like commodities exchanges, the use of programmed trading is one way to work out in advance what actions will be taken. The market moves quickly, and fund managers don't wait until conditions get so good or so bad that the action is obvious to the unaided intuition. By that point, the action would be too late, anyway. Instead, they work out in advance the specific conditions that will trigger a trade and they specify exactly what the trade should be. These instructions are the program that is followed—usually with no further human intervention. The lack of human intervention and the cascade effect of lots of programmed trades causing big market swings has given pro-grammed trading a bad reputation—but this does not have to be the case with program-assisted decisions by humans in business.

Another example in business where specific actions based on real-time information are defined in advance is in statistical process control (SPC). Widely used in manufacturing, SPC requires managers to define "control limits" for each measurement of a process. These manufacturing-related measurements could be about the small variations in the size or color of a part being produced or a defect rate. The control limits might consist of an upper control limit (UCL) and a lower control limit (LCL), which set constraints on how far a measurement can wander before some action is taken. Measurements are monitored continuously during manufacturing processes, and if either the UCL or LCL is breached, alarm bells go off and specific, previously defined actions are taken.

During a rocket launch, during emergency braking in a car with antilock brakes, or during the certain emergency shutdown procedures of a nuclear power plant, we accept that human judgment would not be fast enough or accurate enough. We rely on working out detailed instructions in advance that deal with changing situations, and we make the action an automatically executed procedure. Of course, most business decisions don't necessarily have to be executed in fractions of a second. But in many situations, the amount of time we would have waited to react to data is long after when such a decision would have been optimal.

The decision to cancel a new product launch, to take new security measures, to radically modify a major new project, or to invest in a new technology can be complex and often is based on changing information. Managers might track project completion, sales, inventory levels, or com-modity prices on a frequent, if not quite real-time, basis in order to make these decisions. If those decisions were based on the exploratory mea-surement approach, they might be too late, made without proper analysis, or both.

To determine how well a decision was made in a dynamic environment and to identify possible improvements for the future, it is sometimes worth doing what I call a *forensic* decision analysis. In a forensic decision analysis, we ask at least these types of questions:

- Was the decision in agreement with what would have been decided with a deliberate and detailed analysis?
- What information did managers have that caused an override of a pre-vious direction?
- If the decision was justified, would there have been a benefit to making it earlier?

- If the decision was justified and if there was a benefit to making it earlier, how long did the ideal conditions and the available information exist before managers decided to act on it?
- What were the opportunity losses due to the lag time before the decision was made?
- Would more information have come available if managers waited longer? If so, what would have been the value in waiting?

The point of this exercise is not simply finding fault with past decisions. It is to improve future decisions. And if you applied forensic decision analysis in your organization, you probably would find that most big, course-changing decisions were based on information that was available weeks, months, or perhaps even years prior. If there was a benefit to that decision, and the same conclusion could have been reached much earlier, the costs of the decision lag were the benefits lost during that time.

Now, often there could have been a benefit in waiting, too. But was a particular decision delayed just because managers had already worked out the ideal trigger conditions in advance and were waiting for the optimal conditions to appear? If someone had done the necessary analysis first, it is possible that the delay was deliberate, informed, and rational. However, this is highly unlikely for most decisions. It is much more likely that the optimal time to make the decision was long past and that the delay—and the opportunity loss of the delayed decision—was entirely avoidable.

The difference between the exploratory approach and the programmed, decision-focused approach is not that decisions *couldn't* be defined in advance in the case of exploratory measurement—it is just that they *weren't*. If managers find some set of measures interesting but it looks like they are going to treat the measurements as purely exploratory, I ask:

- Why do you care about these measurements? What decisions would be made differently if this measurement was surprisingly high or surprisingly low?
- What is the "threshold" of this measurement? That is, where is the point where, if this value exceeded it or failed to exceed it, you would engage in an alternative action? For example, if the positive buzz on Twitter about a new product drops, how far would it have to drop before you took action?

The value of a real-time estimate of public mood, economic conditions, or the popularity of a product is fully exploited only if we attempt to work out at least some decision scenarios in advance. If you wait for something out of the ordinary to occur with your dashboard metrics and *then* start to worry about what the measurement means and how you should react, you may as well not worry about using real-time data. You would be just as well off waiting for some regular monthly report based on large and deliberate surveys and hoping you aren't missing too many opportunities in the meantime.

But moving from the exploratory measurement paradigm to the decision measurement paradigm is no more difficult that just asking what you would do in different situations. As an example of this kind of thinking, here is the kind of conversation an analyst might have with a manager who wants to track a new set of data:

Manager: I think it would be interesting to measure the positive-to-negative buzz (P/N) ratio from Twitter on each of our new products, each of our competitors, and also to forecast consumer spending.

Analyst: That sounds very interesting. What will you do with this information?

Manager: It would help us develop a feel for which products we should discontinue, which to promote more vigorously, or even if we need to develop something new.

Analyst: Okay, but when would you do that? How bad would the positive-to-negative buzz ratio on a product need to be before you promote it differently or discontinue it?

Manager: It depends on lots of factors. Maybe if sales have fallen below a certain point but consumer spending is increasing, negative buzz about the specific product might be to blame. Maybe we should fix something about the product or maybe it's just a fundamental demographic shift or change in tastes, and we should discontinue the product.

Analyst: Great! So let's try to spell out those factors and model them now so we don't waste critical time analyzing them after you decided you need to react. Let's just imagine that the P/N ratio of product X dropped from 1.2 to 0.4 in the last year. Do alarm bells sound yet?

Manager: Absolutely. We would definitely have to do something.

Analyst: What would you do? And how much smaller could the change in the P/N ratio be to just barely justify the same action?

Manager: We would have to do some analysis to see how much the P/N ratio would need to change before action was justified. And to determine the action, we would see if it was because of specific recurring complaints, the entry of a competitor's product, the pricing, or something else.

Analyst: Okay, it sounds like that investigation could take a while once the situation occurred. Given the importance of this decision, we better map it out now. What if we also tracked buzz about competitor products and one product had an increasing P/N. We could use that data together with the P/N's for our products as well as our sales in a model of the decision to . . .

At some point the analyst should get to some actual calculations to determine the optimal actions under different conditions. Ideally, this kind of discussion would eventually lead to some well-defined actions with well-defined sets of triggers. This way, at least some major decisions that depend on real-time data can be defined in advance.

This conversation could just as easily started out as a discussion about security using threat analysis of blog-sentiment. Or it could have been a decision to accelerate or terminate a project to build a new facility based on the Pulse of econometric data. Or it could have been the decision to pull or modify an advertising campaign, new legislation, or new product R&D. It could have been a decision to ramp up the inventory of flu vaccine in Atlanta based on early Pulse indications of an outbreak in that area.

No matter which of these decisions it was, there would be a cost of unnecessary decision-lag whether it be missed business opportunities or late reactions to public health threats. With the right metrics to watch (both traditional sources and the Pulse) and the proper trigger conditions defined there would be no decision-lag when the conditions became ripe for a particular action. The entire benefit of that action could be exploited because of timely response to real-time data. Then the Pulse can be harnessed to its full potential.

A Brief Overview of the Economics of Timely Information

Since we need to approach the use of Pulse information within the context of one or more business decisions, just a little bit of background in a discipline called *decision theory* is in order. Decision theory is a mathematical and practical body of knowledge for modeling decisions in order to find optimal strategies, even in highly uncertain situations. Most of my business is building these sorts of decision models for highly uncertain decisions. The models are usually based on Monte Carlo simulations, an important method for assessing the probability of various outcomes—such as the return on investment for a proposed project—when many or all of the inputs are also uncertain.

I use a particular combination of methods from the decision sciences that I call Applied Information Economics (AIE). If you or your firm has a background in quantitative methods for decision analysis, you can skip the next explanation. If you are unfamiliar with these methods, I'll show the key concepts here. See the book's Web site at www.pulsethenewscience.com for additional examples. If you are interested in learning more about the details of AIE, I encourage you to read my first book, *How to Measure Anything: Finding the Value of Intangibles in Business* (hereafter, *HTMA*).

A key part of decision analysis with the AIE method is adopting a more useful definition of measurement as it pertains to decisions under uncertainty. As I mentioned in Chapter 3, in *HTMA* I use a definition for measurement that may be unfamiliar to many managers in business or government but is closer to the de facto use of the word in the sciences. I proposed that a measurement is *a set of observations that reduce uncertainty about a quantity*.[1] This is a much more pragmatic definition, and it recognizes that the point of measurement is uncertainty reduction, not necessarily uncertainty elimination.

If you make any kind of decision that might be influenced by a government report or even your own traditional surveys, then you have to wait for the information. There are pros and cons to waiting. An advantage might be that if you wait longer, your survey could be bigger and the information might be better; or perhaps you wait more to see if market conditions are ripe for the investment. The disadvantage of waiting longer for the information is that you have to defer your decision. This delay can significantly reduce the value of the information.

The Pulse is imperfect, but so are all measures. The question the decision maker has to answer is not whether a measure is perfect, it is whether the benefits of the information were greater than the cost of the information. In *HTMA*, I spent three chapters on quantifying uncertainty and computing the value of information to reduce uncertainty, but I will cover it just briefly here. (See "Key Information Value Concepts for Real-Time Measurements.") For now, just think of the value of information as the reduction in the cost of uncertainty. The cost of uncertainty is a quantity called the expected opportunity loss (EOL) which is, simply put, the cost of being wrong times the chance of being wrong.

When we measure some variable relevant to a decision, uncertainty about that variable is reduced; therefore, overall uncertainty of the decision is reduced, and the EOL is reduced. That reduction in EOL is known as the expected value of information (EVI). This value has to be compared to the expected cost of information (ECI). If it were possible to eliminate all uncertainty, we would have perfect information and the value of that is the expected value of perfect information (EVPI). The EVI can never exceed EVPI.

Key Information Value Concepts for Real-Time Measurements

Measurement: Observations that reduce uncertainty about a quantity. This is much closer to the practical, scientific sense of the term, as distinct from more common definitions like "assigning a value."

Expected opportunity loss (EOL): This is the result of a calculation that, in its simplest form, is the cost of being wrong times the chance of being wrong. In decisions where early timing is important, the opportunity loss can include the forgone benefits from a delayed decision.

Expected value of information (EVI): This is the expected reduction in EOL due to a measurement. Both the amount of uncertainty reduced (measured statistically) and the early timing of the information affect the value of the information.

Expected value of perfect information (EVPI): The EVPI is the maximum value of the EVI (i.e., the value of eliminating all uncertainty). It is equal to the EOL.

Expected cost of information (ECI): This is the amount a proposed measurement is expected to cost. It includes such costs as data gathering (as in a random customer survey) and the cost of analysis. In the case of the Pulse, the cost of gathering more tweets, more eBay transactions, or more network data from Facebook may be negligible. The primary cost may be the overhead of setting up data-gathering algorithms and the analysis.

The more the uncertainty reduction we get from a measure, the higher the EVI. But the longer we have to wait for the information, the lower the value of exploiting it for some decision. The costs of information also tend to go up as measurements become more precise. If you survey more people, for example, you have to spend more money. But the ECI for the Pulse may consist mostly of overhead costs of data retrieval and analysis. The cost of sampling 10 million tweets is not significantly different from the cost of sampling 10,000 tweets. Therefore, we can ignore the effect of ECI for now.

There is actually a quantitative approach for computing EVI. If you have some quantitative background, you will be familiar with these concepts. For those who would like more details, see a spreadsheet on www.pulsethenewscience.com. For now, you can focus on developing a visual understanding of these concepts.

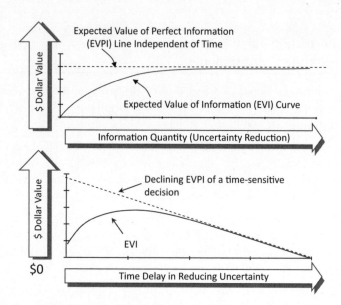

EXHIBIT 9.1   Expected Value of Information versus Waiting
EVI with and without decision-delay considerations

In Exhibit 9.1, I show the EVI under two conditions. In the top chart, EVI increases rapidly then levels off as more information is gathered and uncertainty is reduced. A small amount of uncertainty reduction tends to add a lot of value at first but since the EVI cannot exceed the EVPI, the value of further uncertainty reduction must level off. The top chart makes no mention of uncertainty reduction as a function of time.

In the bottom chart, I consider the effect of opportunity loss from a delay in the decision. As in the first chart, the EVI gets closer to the EVPI as we gather more information. But, in this case, the EVPI is falling as we delay the decision. We could always wait for more information to make a better decision, but the value of making the best decision is falling as time goes by. If we act too soon while uncertainty is still high, the odds of making the wrong decision are higher. There is a "sweet spot" on this curve where it levels off. The value of waiting has maxed out and it is time to act. When we consider a situation where a decision depends on constantly changing information, such as the price of copper or the P/N ratio of sentiment on Twitter about the economy, we always have the option to wait a little bit longer and reduce our uncertainty further. Of course, at some point we know whether our market forecast was right or whether a new product succeeded or failed. But that is known for certain only in hindsight; by that point, the opportunity to exploit the market or modify a new product in some way has passed or is at least greatly reduced.

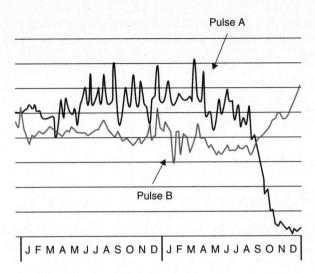

Pulse A

Pulse B

J F M A M J J A S O N D | J F M A M J J A S O N D

EXHIBIT 9.2 **Hypothetical Pulse Readings**

Visualizing the EVI this way is useful, even if we skim over the details of the math. Doing the math, however, often leads to additional revelations. We often find that the maximum part of the EVI curve is surprisingly early. The point of diminishing returns on additional information is reached sooner than our unaided intuition usually would lead us to believe. The other reason I recommend learning to do an information value calculation is that, when I do this calculation, I almost always find that what clients thought they needed to measure and what they really needed to measure were two different things. In *HTMA*, I called this phenomenon the *measurement inversion*.

Now, consider the chart in Exhibit 9.2. Using the Pulse, you were tracking two hypothetical trends over the last two years. Perhaps Pulse A is the P/N ratio from Twitter on one of your products and B is the ratio on a competitor's product. Or perhaps A is Amazon books sales about investing and B is the frequency of searches on terms related to unemployment. Perhaps they are indicators related to a new flu outbreak. If these ratios tell us something about the attractiveness of opening up a new market, expanding operations, or initiating a major public health response, the time to act is slipping away fast, if it is not already gone. At what point would the EVI have been maximized and enough information is at hand to commit to a plan?

Even without getting into some of the quantitative details, this sort of thinking applies to any dynamic information source that affects business decisions, whether it is a commodity price, consumer spending, or customer complaints. If you don't model big decisions in this way now and define triggers for action, you should start doing so, even if you aren't using the Pulse. But doing so is particularly important if you want to get the most out of the Pulse.

Overcoming Cultural and Conceptual Obstacles: Maximizing the Value of the Pulse

The benefits of understanding these ideas are not unique to using the Internet for tracking macro-trends, but they are particularly important in this case. The concept of measurement and the value of information may be unfamiliar to some managers and analysts, but I don't believe these ideas will be a major obstacle for most people. I've trained many hundreds of managers and analysts, and, eventually, they all seem to grasp these ideas intuitively. The bigger obstacle is that they may need to change a bit of culture about decisions in dynamic environments.

One cultural barrier is just the very acceptance of data like blogs and Google searches as inputs to critical decisions. Hopefully, the discussion in Chapter 3 (the section titled "Proving the Pulse: Addressing Misconceptions about the Data") can help. Analysts and managers should study my arguments in that chapter as well as the material in this chapter about the value of information and real-time decisions. They should review the overwhelming evidence published in respected, peer-reviewed scientific journals that the Pulse actually tracks and even forecasts several kinds of economic and social trends. They also should be able to explain why the validity of these studies is not overturned simply because people sometimes use the Internet for silly reasons and that users are not a uniform representation of all age groups or income levels. Still, I offer no magic solutions for converting someone who insists that, contrary to the research shown so far, Internet data cannot possibly be valid. In some cases, people may just have to try employing some aspect of the Pulse to see how well it tracks with forecasts critical to some business decision.

Another possible cultural barrier is the idea of using real-time data in programmed decisions. As discussed, using some version of programmed decisions is the best way to capitalize on dynamic information that affects time-critical decisions. However, managers are wary of anything that they think might take them out of the decision loop. This concern is unjustified, because, for one thing, the models simply produce *recommendations* to managers. There is no need to assume that such information would be used in an automated fashion without any chance of human intervention. Another reason that concern is unjustified is because often the idea that a manager's common sense outperforms a good model is itself an illusion.

Paul Meehl (1920–2003), one of the truly revolutionary researchers in the decision sciences, compared over 150 different statistical models based on historical data to the intuitive judgments of experts. These were judgments as diverse as predicting the outcomes of sporting events, prognosis of liver disease, assessing which candidates would do better in a job, or determining the suicide risk of psychiatric patients. He found that in all but a few cases, the statistical models based on historical data were better at predicting outcomes than the human expert.[2] In fact, in situations where human managers could override the model's recommendation, the humans tended to make things worse.

When Meehl first presented his work in the classic decision science text, *Clinical vs. Statistical Predictions*,[3] it was thoroughly disruptive in several professions. Experts of all stripes were incensed by his findings. How could any statistical model—sometimes a very simple one—capture the qualitative breadth, the subjective complexities, indeed the holistic multitude of factors in their decisions? At about this point, Meehl might have rolled his eyes. He had all the data to back up his claims, and, of course, the experts had never actually measured how well their intuition performed relative to a mathematical model based on historical data. They just *knew* Meehl had to be wrong about the value of their judgment.

Instead of fighting a losing battle with measurable facts about the limits of subjective decision making, managers should focus on the areas where there truly is no substitute for human cognition: the definition of problems, the identification of influential factors, and articulating a hypothesis to be tested. Even the most mathematically rigorous of the physical sciences rely entirely on human intuition to do this. Once the problem is defined and measurements are identified, the scientist generally knows to concede to the quantitative measures instead of subjective intuition. In fact, managers should feel their role is elevated by removing themselves from routine tactical decisions. Their expertise is best used if they focus on the more strategic activity of managing decision models instead of individual, tactical decisions.

There may also be conceptual obstacles for analysts to overcome. I've written in the past about what I think is a pervasive culture among the profession of quantitative business analysts that the only path to better analysis is better tinkering with models and ever more exhaustive analysis of data internal to the firm.[4] Certainly, almost any quantitative model can be improved by further tinkering. And, no doubt, there is more to be learned by examining from even more angles the sometimes gigantic databases of modern organizations. However, this extensive tinkering is almost always done to the point of diminishing returns and then some. The underutilized strategy is identifying high-value measurements and making structured observations like a scientist.

Many quantitative analysts, or "quants," are already familiar with the details of these concepts. Skills related to proper empirical analysis will be critical in getting the most out of the Pulse—or, for that matter, getting the most out of the data the organization already has in its databases. So I would like to encourage my quant colleagues to look up periodically from their models and attempt some empirical measurements that would serve as inputs to the models as well as validate the output of the models. Science does involve models, but it also involves empirical observation. Measurements based on the Pulse would be useless without the kind of scientific validation done by the scientists in Chapters 5, 6, and 7.

Implementing the Pulse

I keep saying that the sexy job in the next ten years will be statisticians and data analysts. People think I'm joking, but who would've guessed that computer engineers would've been the sexy job of the 1990s?—Hal Varian, Google chief economist, 2009, in an interview with *The McKinsey Quarterly*

It is useful for managers to think of the Pulse as a greatly extended form of what they may recognize as business intelligence (BI), predictive analytics (PA), or executive dashboards. Recall from the first three chapters that many organizations have adopted BI, PA, and dashboard tools, but the tools almost entirely look inward at an organization's own database. Still, the basic objective of BI, PA, and dashboards is the same if implemented with the Pulse. The point is still to condense and present a large, complex, and rapidly changing data set to forecast outcomes and make better decisions. Here is a five-step process I propose to implement the Pulse with existing kinds of business tools and with decision-focused measurements:

1. *Define and model decisions.* Identify specific decisions that could be informed by the Pulse or any other BI. Any class of decisions in the organization—including project approval, operational decisions, advertising campaigns, and so on—are candidates. For each decision, we identify the high-value measurements for them and their trigger values/control limits.
2. *Identify possible tracking and forecasting methods.* These forecasts feed the decision models. They could include macroeconomic forecasts, the risks of a pandemic, the adoption rates of new technologies, actions of competitors, and others.

3. *Identify sources of this information.* Sources may be internal proprietary information or something that can be gleaned from the Pulse.
4. *For data coming from the Internet, design data capture methods for each of the data sources.* Methods may employ a combination of Application Program Interfaces (APIs), screen-scrapers, and third-party providers of Internet data. This information is dumped to formats that are accessible by BI, PA, or other tools for analyzing data.
5. *Iteratively run components of the forecasting and decision models and check them against observed outcomes.* Models are refined and new information sources are constantly being investigated.

When these steps are implemented, the result should look something like Exhibit 9.3. This is a continuous process; even though you start in the definition of decisions, decisions are shown here as part of the whole loop.

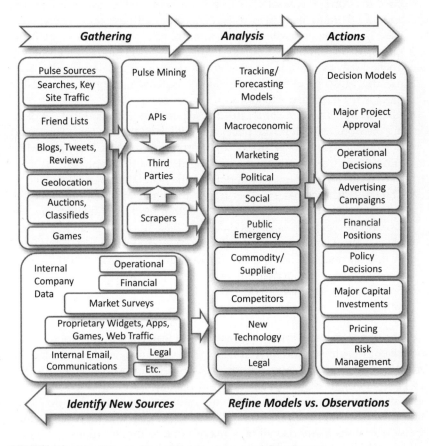

EXHIBIT 9.3   The Pulse as Part of the Decision-Modeling Process

As the bottom of Exhibit 9.3 shows, a valid use of the Pulse depends on a constant state of validation and calibration. We *never* take for granted that a hypothetical relationship between the Pulse and real-world phenomenon is a fact. We conclude it to be a fact only after we have shown that the relationship correlates closely with verified outcomes and that the observed relationship is highly unlikely to be due to chance alone. Like the scientists discussed in earlier chapters, we have to confirm models against outcomes. The only difference is that business will perform this checking on a continuous-process basis.

To exploit this new tool, organizations will need new players or at least slightly modified roles in place. Some of the new roles include:

- *Business intelligence analyst.* The BI analysts in organizations today need to evolve a new set of skills related to Internet information sources and add them to skills in statistical analysis methods and decision analysis. These analysts will start out in fairly low positions in many organizations but should eventually evolve toward positions of influence. These analysts are in charge of the forecasting models (whether they use the Pulse or internal information sources) and building decision models for particular situations.
- *Internet intelligence technicians.* These people are in charge of developing methods to retrieve the necessary data from the Internet. They must be familiar with APIs, scrapers, and third-party sources. They should be familiar with their company's existing database platform and BI tools so that there is a seamless interface in the accessibility of all data.
- *Chief intelligence officer.* This is not the chief information officer or the chief technology officer, both of whom tend to be entirely inward looking in regard to business data. The best analogy for a chief intelligence officer in the current business organization is perhaps the head of market research, as it is at least outward looking in its orientation. But the chief intelligence officer also keeps a look out for risks and opportunities on the horizon.

The use of the new Pulse information will lead to new kinds of decision models for businesses and governments. The management decision-making process is perhaps the most critical yet most unimproved frontier for better productivity. If management decision making is still unresponsive and error-prone, the value of faster and better information is virtually zero. Combining the real-time, outward-looking Pulse with better and more responsive decision analysis methods will be a major boon to organizations.

Notes

1. D. Hubbard. *How to Measure Anything: Finding the Value of Intangibles in Business.* 2nd ed. (Hoboken, NJ: John Wiley & Sons, 2010).
2. P.E. Meehl. *Clinical Versus Statistical Prediction: A Theoretical Analysis and a Review of the Evidence*, Minneapolis: University of Minnesota Press, 1954, pp. 372–373.
3. Ibid.
4. D. Hubbard and D. Samuelson. "Modeling Without Measurements: How the Decision Analysis Culture's Lack of Empiricism Reduces Its Effectiveness." *OR/MS Today.* October 2009, www.lionhrtpub.com/orms/orms-10-09/frrisk.html.

CHAPTER 10

The Future of the Pulse and Its New Challenges

By the 2030s, the non-biological portion of our intelligence will predominate.

—Ray Kurzweil, *The Singularity is Near*, 2005

The future ain't what it used to be.

—Yogi Berra

On my bookshelf is a copy of the magazine *Popular Science* from April 1962, the month I was born. In it is an article titled "What'll It Be Like in 2000 A.D.?" As you might guess, this attempt at predicting life in the future didn't get everything right. In 2000, we were not driving down automated highways that drove our cars for us and our cars certainly weren't flying around. Still, the article did get some things right. It mentioned that computers would be talking to each other, and it even foretold flat-panel TVs and video communications. In other ways, the predictions fell short of reality. In the article, the primary function of computers talking to each other was apparently to control household appliances and banking. The ubiquity of hand-held phones with powerful computers was not imagined; nor did the author foresee social networks, blogs, Wikipedia, or YouTube. Who could have, back in 1962?

A futurist doesn't have to get everything right. Instead, I think exercises to identify future possibilities should be thought of as a portfolio of ideas. Like the 1962 article in *Popular Science,* some predictions will pay off; others may not. However, almost any combination of ideas coming to fruition will produce incredible opportunities. The fact that it is possible to get even some predictions right is what should motivate us to prepare for changes.

The best predictions tend to be those where the fundamental nature of people and systems, unchanging as they are, lead to foreseeable results,

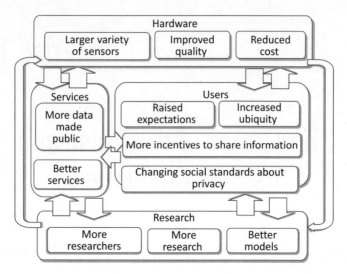

EXHIBIT 10.1   Accelerating Feedback Cycle of the Pulse

even if only in the broadest sense. If we see several things we all agree are inevitable, then we should look at what the implications of those things in are in many combinations. Then we find consequences of those inevitabilities that must also be inevitable.

One fundamentally unchanging aspect of humanity is that we can always count on people to act in their own best interest. It is also not too much of a leap to state that the research into the Pulse has just begun and that models will continue to improve. In addition, we are fairly certain that technology will continue to improve.

The future will involve changing society, changing services, changing models, and changing hardware. I believe these fundamental, structural aspects of the Pulse will create a positive feedback loop where each iteration amplifies the effect of the next. Exhibit 10.1 depicts how I imagine them each feeding off each other and causing an accelerating rate of change.

Users and the Data They Share Will Increase

The most important component of the Pulse—the users who provide information—will continue to evolve in multiple ways. There will be more users and they will be more diverse. They will probably spend more time on the Internet, they will probably be willing to reveal more of certain kinds of information, and their expectations for the availability of information will increase.

We know that, however Internet users change or however the Internet changes, there will definitely be more Internet users. As shown in Chapter 3, the number and diversity of users has expanded from a specialized group of a few million to 2 billion people in the span of a single generation. And while the majority of users in the developed world have both Internet access and mobile phones, the developing world has plenty of room to grow. The growth in Internet and mobile phone use will be driven by both reduced costs and increased benefits of being an Internet user. In particular, the improving functionality and reduced costs of mobile devices and their features will accelerate their usage.

Users will spend more time on the Internet and will be more willing (albeit with some caveats) to reveal more of their personal information. The amount of time spent per user per week on the Internet, as shown in Chapter 3, grew steadily until 2009 and then stagnated. This does not mean that users have been saturated in the amount of time they are willing to spend on the Internet. Most of the growth from 2006 to 2009 was due to the appearance of social networking sites. Prior to 2006, the time spent per person looked as if it had already stagnated. People will spend more time as new and better-quality services appear—which they will.

Users will also be more willing, in some ways, to divulge the kind of information that will be useful for the Pulse. This is due in part because incentives to share information probably will increase as services develop useful features that require the information. Another reason people may become more likely to share some information is simply because, in some respects, concepts of privacy are changing. The idea of privacy has not disappeared, but the demand for it is evolving in complex ways.

Some in the news have used the outright exhibitionist behavior of many young people on social networks as evidence of a drastic shift in attitudes toward privacy. However, these anecdotes exaggerate and oversimplify the change in expectations regarding privacy. The following results from some privacy research paint a more elaborate picture of our attitudes toward privacy:

- One study about privacy attitudes does show that there are more relaxed privacy attitudes among the young, but the difference is very slight.[1] Part of that finding showed that the differences in attitudes toward privacy might simply be differences in knowledge about privacy rights. In some ways, we are actually becoming more aware of privacy concerns, and we are just becoming more practical about privacy.
- A 2007 Australian study found that, compared to 2001, more Australians were willing to divulge information about income, health, and even their genetics but less willing to provide information such as home address or phone number.[2] The study found that refusals to reveal information due

to objections based on principle (e.g., like "It's none of their business" or "It's an invasion of privacy") decreased from 51% to 36% in that time period. On the other hand, practical concerns, such as potential threats to finances, personal safety, or being bothered by junk mail or spam, were becoming much more relevant.

- Incentives matter when it comes to the willingness to share information, but they have to be the right incentives. The Australian study showed that fewer people were willing to disclose personal information in 2007 than in 2001 if they were offered a discount on a purchase or chance to win a prize.

- An interesting caveat we should consider with the Australian study is that it was not based on actual behavior but stated preferences about the willingness to share information. As we saw in Chapter 8, revealed preferences (what people actually do) and stated preferences are often not the same. A 2007 study in the *Journal of Consumer Affairs* found that people actually shared information at a consistently higher rate than what they said they would in surveys.[3] The survey-based Australian study may understate what people would actually share in practice.

- Health and safety do appear to be effective incentives. Another study showed that people who are more concerned with their health are also more willing to reveal health information.[4] And as we saw in Chapter 8, one incentive for revealing personal information like location has been a crisis where health and safety are at risk.

- Socializing seems to be sufficient to incentivize quite a lot of us to share information. The popularity of certain location-based apps like Yelp, Foursquare, and Google Goggles indicates that the features of these apps are reason enough for many people to share their locations.

- At least some of us seem to be willing to provide information for the sake of science. The Framingham Heart Study (first mentioned in Chapter 6) showed how large groups of people can be motivated to provide information if they believe it is for a greater good. In a related example, thousands of people have volunteered their own computers, while the computers would otherwise have been idle, for massive public distributed computing projects. By distributing computational problems among thousands of volunteered computers, astronomers have been crunching numbers on such big problems as the search for pulsars[5] and even in the search for extraterrestrial intelligence.[6]

Keep in mind that not all privacy concerns are matters of public display of information. Is the privacy of individual buyers of books on Amazon violated when Amazon publishes the sales ranks of books? Or does a map of traffic flow on the expressways violate the privacy of individual drivers? Highly aggregated information like this is not, in itself, a privacy issue. As long as users trust the information aggregator, revealing aggregated data is not the same as publishing individual physical locations or purchases for the world to see.

Furthermore, not all users necessarily need to be willing to reveal this information in order for it to be useful. Recall from Chapters 4 and 5 that millions of people have downloaded the Alexa toolbar. In exchange for the toolbar's search features, Alexa tracks in great detail where those users are going to on the Internet and how long they stay. Only a small fraction of 1% of Internet users have decided to download the Alexa toolbar—and that is more than enough for the Pulse.

Probably the most important characteristic of human behavior for the Pulse is that once people's expectations are raised, it is very hard for them to retract the new standard. As mentioned in Chapter 3, a majority of people worldwide actually believe Internet access—something most didn't have a generation ago—is a basic human right. If expectations about what we all have a right to can change that much that fast, then we should not be surprised if other major shifts in expectations occur as new features are available on the Internet and mobile phones. Once people get something, they expect to keep getting it, and they would rebel if they didn't. These increasing expectations impact services provided, the kind of research that can be done, and the incentives to develop new technologies.

Services Will Be Better and Make More Data Public

Service providers will come and go, but the general incentives of service providers will not. As hard as it is to imagine that services like Google, Facebook, or Amazon, might go away, we can't take for granted that they will always be here. The total time spent per week on the social site Myspace was much more than what was spent on Amazon or eBay before it rapidly diminished.

One aspect of service providers that remains remarkably stable is the distribution patterns of traffic among sites. As shown in Chapter 4, the share of traffic allocated to the big sites follows Zipf's law, and this basic pattern has not changed in nearly a decade of Internet growth. It probably will always be the case that relatively few major services will produce most of the data for the Pulse. Another dynamic that will not change is competition driven by users' increased expectation of novelty and features. And as already pointed out, users' expectations have a kind of ratchet effect—once they go up, it is hard for them to go down.

Services such as Facebook, eBay, or Amazon eventually may decide to aggregate and then display information they currently have but don't share. The dynamics of data sharing are an unconventional sort of economics, but, from what we have seen so far, there appears to be some kind of motivation for services to make data public even when doing so doesn't appear to offer a direct benefit to the service firm.

For example, Google did not have to produce Google Trends, and Twitter did not have to release its Firehose Application Program Interface (API). But they did, and such services are becoming expected. As already pointed out, service providers can cancel what they previously gave away only at some cost to public relations if not direct business. Also, the availability of information quickly creates an ecosystem of supporting services that are more than just inconvenienced when the information is then no longer available. They do what they have to in order to stay in business. For example, as pointed out in Chapter 4, when Amazon's APIs stopped providing access to Kindle data, developers just went back to HTML scraping.

Even without the threat of HTML scrapers, some data is made freely available. Unlike the data offered by eBay, Amazon, and Twitter, the Google Trends data could not have been obtained by HTML scrapers, so Trends was not offered out of concern for unwanted loads on the server—in fact, Google Trends gives Google's infrastructure even more to do. And Google has no legal obligations to continue providing Google Trends. The relationship of Trends to Google's revenue (advertising) is highly indirect, at best. Perhaps the only reason for Google to show its search volume data is that the types of talent that Google likes to hire feel motivated by an atmosphere of experimentation with services like Trends. But if this service disappeared, especially after people and businesses got used to having it, there probably would be a public relations cost.

Because of increasing user expectations, not only is it hard for services to discontinue what they already offer, it may become more expected for other sites to release information in the same way that Google and Twitter have. Twitter can't release more if only because it already releases everything—that is, every single tweet in real-time streams. But most other sites could make more available and provide them in APIs or direct downloads. Here are a few examples to illustrate the potential:

- Google currently tracks only a subset of all search terms on Google Trends. Many searches in Google Trends now produce a message that your search terms "do not have enough search volume to show graphs." Of course, even the low-volume data can be used if you purchase Adwords. But it probably would not be difficult for Google to track a much larger set of search terms, if it sets its mind to it.
- Game sites that do reveal aggregate data about game-play reveal only a tiny fraction of the data they have. Ostensibly, the reluctance to reveal this detail is so that players couldn't exploit the data for gaming purposes. But even some highly aggregated form of this data could be a boon to social scientists. What if gamers received points for participating in surveys before each game session or for volunteering data from

other online activities? This would be a way to gather large-scale data about how income status, relationship status, anxiety, and more affect game play in detail. I like the idea of a "risk-taking index" based on the percentage of players taking certain actions in the game that result in death. As previously mentioned research has shown, attitudes in game play reflect something about real life.

- Map sites like MapQuest or Google Maps could produce *planned* traffic maps based on the directions people are seeking. The route provided doesn't necessarily mean that a person actually will use it or even go to that destination. Drivers may seek directions to a destination just before they leave or days in advance as part of some more extensive travel planning. Perhaps users would be willing to enter their expected travel time in exchange for forecasted traffic data.

- Traffic counters on Web sites have become passé (remember the "number of visitors to this site" counters that seemed so common in the 1990s?), but it might be a good idea for, say, government sites to renew them as a retro fad. Perhaps state services sites could report, real time, not just overall traffic (which can be retrieved now from Alexa) but which particular pages people spent the most time on. This information would all be in the aggregate, of course. (The state wouldn't report what a particular identified visitor did.) For example, the data would tell us only that there was a 15% increase since last month in people reading about foreclosure laws or a 28% increase in traffic to the page with contact information for the office that handles auto dealer complaints. It is *our* data, after all.

- Wikipedia, the free crowd-sourced Internet encyclopedia, is one of the top sites on the Internet, but it currently produces only infrequent and limited reports on the popularity of articles. As a not-for-profit organization, Wikipedia is the ideal sort of service to be motivated by the research potential of near-real-time reporting of traffic to articles. An increased popularity in articles related to real estate, construction, and home improvement could signal increased planning for investment in that area. Increased traffic to a page about a political figure could correlate to the politician's popularity. We would just have to have access to the data to test these potential relationships.

- Retail sites and, in particular, Amazon could make it easier to estimate sales by category. Instead of posting sales rank, Amazon could just indicate a rate of sales for each book. Or it could simply reveal its sales rank formula. One possible reason Amazon might not do so is because the formula might show how mediocre most book sales really are. (Do you *really* want to know that you are only the second person to buy a book that has been published for three years?) It might also reveal that parts of the algorithm are a bit arbitrary. (How much should the rank change due to new sales versus past sales?) However, these are already not secrets. Also, other major retailers might get some publicity mileage out of similar product rankings. Imagine the "Wal-Mart Home Improvement Index" based on sales of items correlated to home improvement or the "Target Christmas Index" based on sales of items more likely to be given as gifts. These statistics could be as relevant to measuring the economy as the Dow Jones Industrial Average, and they could merit more publicity if media outlets came to report such information regularly.

These examples are of sites presenting aggregate forms of data they already have, but services will also have new data, and they may have similar pressures to release it in some aggregate form to the public. If they can develop new, innovative services, people will be more willing to volunteer more information. Areas ripe for major improvements in the functionality of services include what could be reaped from more location sharing using mobile phones and more sharing of text and voice communications (not the individual communications, only aggregated forms):

- A map of the social scene in a city can provide hints for where more interesting people might be met based on locations of other people using their apps. Instead of matching potential friends or relationship-based self-reported surveys, inferences about personalities are made from places traveled, friend networks, language used in text, and so on.
- A person could avoid the risk of catching the flu by avoiding high-risk areas. The information about risk is estimated from other users of the flu-avoidance app, and people's chances of illness can be assessed from changes in their movements and communications (as one study described in Chapter 8 showed to be possible).
- If a person plans a route to a theater on a mobile phone app, the app may provide a route that avoids unsafe areas.
- Monitoring your movements and communications, your "executive coach app" makes inferences about your relative effectiveness on different tasks on different days.
- Your "health coach app" leverages the research of Nicholas Christakis (see Chapter 6) to suggest different venues for socializing that are more likely to put you among people who will be more positive influences on your health. It would recommend walking routes that are more physically demanding and psychologically make it more likely to encourage you to stay healthy.

These features will generate new reasons to share data, which will provide better data for research, which will produce new models for even better features.

Research and Models

Research will improve as will the predictive algorithms produced by researchers. The last two years has been only the very beginning of this new era of social science. While researchers have already found convincing evidence of how the buzz on the Internet predicts macro-trends, current researchers are only scratching the surface.

Many thousands of careers are yet to be made in mining important trends from a vast and growing Internet. And more researchers will find more ways to use more data. In every university where I have interviewed people who have done this kind of research, I find graduate students who are avid fans of this emerging field and plan on making a career out of it. The scientific community has gone a long way since Gunther Eysenbach first tried to get his research published. There will be even more scientific conferences and journals dedicated to the topics of the Pulse. New economic forecasts, new social trends and new public health patterns will be discovered from data that may already exist. Many more dissertations and cross-disciplinary collaborations will form.

It is effectively impossible that everything that can be predicted with our digital footprints has already been determined. An afternoon of brainstorming with dynamic thinkers is enough to generate several fruitful fields of research. To seed the brainstorming, here are some potential areas worth further investigation by the appropriately curious and motivated:

- Would an analysis of people's travel, what they read on the Internet, and patterns of speech tell us something useful about them? I mentioned the possibility of social matchmaking based on passively collected data like this. Perhaps what people actually do is a much better predictor of successful matches than what they say they do on a survey.
- Do movement and communication patterns aggregated for thousands of people in an area predict risks of crime, the spread of disease, or even hazards like fire? The study mentioned in Chapter 8 about how text messages correlated to building damage after the 2010 Haiti earthquake portends other possibilities. What if by tracking location passively via GPS or accelerometers, people fleeing a single area could be observed real time, even before any call for help? What if once they do call for help, they have the option to become a civil defense sensor? (They volunteer their location and their camera in order to get information to authorities quickly.)
- In what ways do the articles and books we read correlate to expected future behaviors? In Chapter 8, I briefly examined whether the popularity of a set of books about getting out of debt might correlate to a larger financial trend. But book sales just scratch the surface. Does an increase in the sales of books about starting a new business or new career say

something about trends in the economy? Do increased sales of books about depression or alcoholism indicate a rise in those afflictions? Or perhaps more people read articles about these topics on Wikipedia or watch more videos about it on YouTube. Many combinations of topics and trends are wide open to investigation.

- Researchers will develop better algorithms for analyzing images, video, and speech. If applied to massive sources of data like Flickr and YouTube, will these tools tell us anything about mood, interests, economics, and health? Perhaps even *backgrounds* of videos and photos tell us something if they show more traffic in retail stores, more smiling or frowning people, or more travel. What would researchers find if we could volunteer all the background noise on our phone that had nothing to do with our own conversation? Could we find happier places by listening for laughter? Would this correlate with health and the economy?

- Perhaps people can enroll in studies on Facebook in the same way they pick up games like Mafia Wars or Farmville. If people enroll in a study, they could be asked to provide additional information that would be of interest to the researchers. Such studies could be purely academic but could also be done for the private sector.

- We have already seen that people are willing to provide a lot of their information and even computer time if they feel they are participating in something for the greater good of science. Many people might be willing to volunteer real-time feeds of certain aspects of their lives if they felt the information was for the greater good and in the hands of trustworthy researchers, and if they were asked to do so.

- Research might find that it is possible to tweak relatively minor aspects of our lives to improve health and performance. The health coach app just mentioned needs a lot of research to see what subtle ways the lives of people can be nudged toward better health if the app has access to real-time data on location, communications, searches, and the like. Research behind the executive coach app would help discover if there are ways to fine-tune our career performance. (I, for one, would like more data on what situations are more likely to make me a more productive writer or consultant.)

- What if simulations could have predicted the increasing body mass index of Americans as a result of daily activities? Imagine a new office in the Centers for Disease Control and Prevention (CDC) watching a Pulse about a particular combination of symptoms being complained about in social media posts and an increase in the number of searches related to flu-like symptoms but with an additional symptom of swollen joints. Perhaps a slightly higher than average number of deaths are being reported as heart attacks but the families of the victims posted on social media similar behavioral changes before the death. Perhaps those deaths correlated with blogs about a new herbal medicine purchase. How long would conventional methods take to even notice such subtleties?

■ Many medical studies rely on Patient Reported Outcomes (PRO), a periodic survey-based method of collecting data about, say, pain experienced by the patient. A detailed tracking of movement (at a micro–time-and-motion level) and communications might be a better way to infer pain than subjective "pain scales" of 1 to 10 points.

■ Researchers will make more use of micropayments for human intelligence tasks (mentioned in Chapter 7). What if someone on Amazon Mechanical Turk was paid a nickel every time they volunteered a photo or video of a crowd that included location data? What if people were paid 50 cents an hour for their detailed tracking of movements and other activities? This is not the kind of randomized trial that most researchers would prefer, but the bias in such studies can be measured and accounted for.

This kind of research will help build models that will have predictive value to government agencies and businesses. And as models improve, they will converge, and convergence fosters more improvement. As models are built, there will be a strong incentive to connect with other decision models from other organizations. For example, if a nuclear power plant is assessing the risk—in real time—of safety-related employee shortages due to a pandemic, it will not develop its own pandemic model; it will simply use the CDC model.

The continuous improvement of these models—following the methods described in Chapter 9—will also feed new academic research. As these models become more effective in their predictive power, organizations will, again, find more reasons to connect to models in other organizations. Just as individuals find reasons to share data, organizations will find reasons to justify sharing their data models with others, as long as it doesn't violate some levels of confidentiality (like customers' credit data) and as long as there is something in it for the organization.

From Communicators to Tricorders—for Everyone

We can also be quite certain that hardware technology will continue to improve and will become cheaper. This is such a worn idea in the last several decades that it may be easy to see it as not so much a prediction but a simple fact. Of particular use to the Pulse will be continued improvements in mobile devices for the average consumer. The ubiquity, variety, and quality of mobile sensors will allow for new data feeds that will only increase the incentive for information sharing.

In the area of continued hardware improvement, science fiction is a useful brainstorming tool. At first, our science fiction analog for the mobile phone has been something like the 1960's version of the *Star Trek* communicator. We flip it open, hit some buttons, and we are talking to Scotty. In episodes from the 1990s we see the characters of *Star Trek: The Next Generation* carrying around flat electronic tablets that seem to function a lot like what we now call iPads or Kindles. And since the original series, the *Star Trek* communicator evolved into a passively worn tracker and health monitor for personnel.

For the Pulse, the most important development will be the hybrid of the communicator and the tricorder. The tricorder was the all-purpose measurement instrument that Spock always seemed to have handy. It could detect many parts of the electromagnetic spectrum and could perform chemical analysis of the environment. Spock only lacked the Internet to continuously dump his tricorder readings to.

This scenario doesn't really seem all that futuristic anymore. Our smartphones can do a lot of tricorder/communicator hybrid functions now and with a little modification could do even more. Think of the microphone, accelerometer, GPS and other components of your phone as a kind of Internet-connected, sensor packet you carry around. These devices will continue to improve in several ways and each improvement opens up new applications. According to trends we are all used to seeing throughout the history of electronic devices, we can count on the continuous improvement in cost, quality and variety of sensors in the mobile devices we carry:

- *Cost of devices.* The cost of some mobile phones and mobile phones with Internet access continues to drop to the point where they can be possessed by those we would normally consider too impoverished to own one. The idea that Internet access is a fundamental human right (as first mentioned in Chapter 3) will only be amplified as devices get even cheaper. And we can count on costs getting so cheap that Internet-connected devices could be as cheap as a pen and smaller than a coin.

- *Quality of sensors.* Resolution of location and other data will improve. The study mentioned in Chapter 8 about using movements to infer illness was a very coarse measure of movement, but it was still adequate for the purpose. The accelerometers in all smartphones could be used for a much more fined-tuned measure of activity.

- *More sensors of different types will be packed into our phones.* The proliferation of cheap sensors that are connected to the Internet for a range of applications will make another series of Pulse tracks possible. Sensors in phones can approximate sensor networks that currently are closed affairs used by government agencies for tracking weather, earthquakes, ocean currents, pollution, traffic, and vibrations of structures. Air-quality sensors in our phones will analyze air for chemical threats, humidity, and even airborne diseases. For the same reasons that other information becomes publicly available on the Internet, incentives will exist to do the same with sensor data. Here are three examples of new types of sensors for feeding the Pulse:

— One imminent, major development will be the implementation of Near Field Communication (NFC). Nokia and Apple have already applied for patents for this technology, which detects nearby, inexpensive wireless tags embedded in objects.[7] For example, an action figure related to an upcoming movie could have a tag embedded inside it, so that bringing an iPhone close the figure would cause the movie trailer to start playing.

— Technology developed by Sonavasion uses a fingerprint-swipe identification method that also detects blood flow (for security purposes, this eliminates the threat where a finger or hand is cut off and used in a scanner). It portends the opportunity for passively gathered health data.

— Some developments simply make better use of existing sensors. Hong Lu, while a PhD candidate at Dartmouth, developed an app called Jigsaw which uses the phone's microphone to pick up ambient noise even when the phone is not on. Detailed daily data is automatically posted to a Facebook page along with data from the accelerometer and GPS devices on the phone. At this point Lu says the device was made for "pure research" but the potential as some form of consumer product is there.

Evolving Opportunities and Challenges for Users of the Pulse

Trends in hardware, acceptance of (and demand for) data sharing, new services and new research will combine in many ways both foreseeable and not. But one foreseeable result is that we will see devices in more places and there will be more per individual. Our interface to the Internet will not be limited to keyboards or mobile phones. Large numbers of tiny, networked sensors could be created for each person and they could be distributed in mundane objects. This idea has been called "smart dust" and it would vastly multiply the ubiquity of sensors and the volume of data. Data will be pouring into the Internet from cars, household appliances, and perhaps even our bodies.

People in health studies may volunteer for implanted forms of various health sensors. I would do that myself if I thought it might help with real-time warnings of heart disease (a problem in my family). This would be an entirely new level of passive data collection that might provide a volume of data even Nicholas Christakis does not yet have available for health studies using computational social science. Perhaps my life insurance company would give me a discount in exchange for the health stream of data. Perhaps an auto insurance company would do the same for those volunteering the real-time streams of sensors in their cars. And once they have this data, researchers and service providers will find more things to do with it.

Perhaps more of what we see, hear, and smell will be fed into the Pulse. As long as a sensor is available, someone will find a reason to give part of this information away in exchange for some benefit. Someone will find a reason to aggregate it and post it in a way that can be exploited for the Pulse. The emerging technology of augmented reality is a natural for two-way information sharing data involving more of our senses. Augmented reality is a way of overlaying information about our environment onto what we see and hear (and perhaps other senses too). Augmented reality will involve wearing unobtrusive eyewear that projects onto our field of view additional information about what we are looking at. For example, we could see the star rating of the restaurant we are walking past, we could see the names of people we know in the crowd. The device might warn you of people at the airport who may have the flu or would be willing to strike up a conversation about furniture making. This may seem like one of the most speculative form of technology discussed, but strides toward it are made every year. The service that gives the augmented reality information has to track your location and where you are looking (very specifically). Tracking these, it also knows speed, acceleration, attention, and so on.

Massive improvements in data storage and data transmission will make it more feasible to track real-time video of the environment and record a large share of a person's life. We may want to track not just time online but "surveillance time." (Surveillance time would be the number of hours per week a person records his or her life.) Why tweet what you are doing now if you can just show it? Of course, most people wouldn't leave their "broadcast my view" switch on all the time. But I'm sure some would just as some are willing to participate in the "big brother" kinds of reality shows. This level of data will make the work of Nathan Eagle and Nicholas Christakis appear coarse in comparison.

And then, of course, the *really* futuristic stuff can begin. Our homes, cars, and even perhaps bodies can change appetites for, say, energy based on prevailing conditions. Sensors in bodies don't have to wait for me to search on Google for flu symptoms in order for the CDC to know there is an outbreak in my neighborhood. Inventory levels will change in part due to close tracking of chatter about your products or raw materials. Police patrol cars will be advised which direction to turn to be in a place where they are *more likely* to avert a crime.

Before the Pulse can be of use to business and government in a major way, we will have to address several challenges unique to this new kind of instrument:

- We know we need to adjust for media and herding behavior. These factors apparently were not a major source of noise in the studies shown in Chapters 5 and 7, but we should be vigilant. We know that some movements are there because people are following the media or the herd and not necessarily because of individual preferences. If we find that lots of people are searching on "unemployment," we know that it may be because they are responding to a flood of media pronouncements about a recent report. Fortunately, we can also measure media coverage and adjust the crowd behavior accordingly. We also know that individuals, not just media outlets, can be very influential and that a cascade effect among influential people can occur independent of media attention.
- We should continue to refine and calibrate Pulse methods by adjusting for outliers and biased selection. It is possible for extreme outliers to drive a measurement of the Pulse and selection of users of the Internet will limit some applications. The fact is that Internet users are not a truly uniform and random representation of the entire population. That fact alone did not stop the Pulse from being an extremely useful measure, or even predictor, of things like unemployment, consumer spending, public health crisis, and opinions—but further improvements are still possible.
- Potentially, malicious actors could learn to manipulate the Pulse. Some of the Pulse could be gamed, especially if it is known that major organizations use this data for big decisions and if there is some way individuals could "arbitrage" the opportunity. But there are strategies to defend against such manipulation and we should assume from the beginning that the Pulse will be a new kind of competition similar to virus/antivirus or terrorist/security competitions. In the past, some have developed methods to manipulate Google with "Google bombs." Google bombs create search traffic in a way that affects Google's anticipation of your search. (At one point, this kind of attack made it so that the search for "French military victories" caused Google to respond "Did you mean French military defeats?") The defense against this kind of manipulation probably will be as simple as using a multitude of sources of information from the Pulse in your own proprietary models. If your model for predicting growth in your industry involves tracking the frequency of 14 different search terms on Google and traffic to 31 specific

Web sites, and you didn't reveal what your model is, it would be hard for a malicious actor to manipulate the Pulse in a way that affects you. And if some of your model involves purchases of a category of items on eBay or books on Amazon, the only way for the model to be maliciously manipulated would be at some significant expense to the manipulators, especially if they didn't know what specific items to buy up.

As previously mentioned, the major service providers will continue to evolve, and some may disappear. Suppose a business depends on a combination of Twitter and Google Trends data for its models, and the models have been calibrated with a few years of data. The business may have modified logistics and marketing in a way that both capitalizes on this model and makes the firm more dependent on it. The best defense against changes in companies who provide services is the same as the defense against malicious actors: Have diversified sets of information sources. Also, a constant state of monitoring various Internet resources as input to the Pulse would be required. (Such a service could be a new business opportunity.) That way, models can be modified dynamically even as players change.

The full effect of these opportunities and issues may be a broader effect on the economy and society as a whole. It may be possible for feedback loops to be stabilizing or destabilizing in the economy. "Positive feedback" is a good term when it comes to employee motivation, but to a systems analyst it could refer to potentially catastrophic results. A "positive feedback" in the controls of an airplane would be disastrous because a slight overcorrection would become a larger overcorrection, then larger still. Also, when the swing of a building matches the resonance of an earthquake, oscillations can increase until the building collapses. The same has been said of programmed trading in the stock market. Irrational exuberance begets more irrational exuberance.

But if there were an "irrational exuberance" indicator, then it could infuse caution into the market just when it is needed. Perhaps the delay in understanding the movement of the crowd is itself part of what causes cycles. Like flying a plane with loose and delayed controls, each action tends to be an overcorrection. Properly utilized, perhaps the Pulse can correct for this. Perhaps the Pulse could eliminate what is assumed by many economists to be a fundamentally unchanging aspect of economics: the existence of economic cycles. More finely tuned monitoring is required for more finely tuned control. If this data were available real-time to everyone, we would not have to wait on periodic government reports.

Meeting these sorts of challenges and exploiting the opportunities will be up to users of the Pulse. We can only imagine what sorts of maps Dr. John Snow (see Chapter 2) might have devised if he had the tools that Christina Corbane (see Chapter 8) had at her disposal. If employers seeking employees or singles seeking a life mate were notified of good matches while they were online or in a train station, how would the aggregated form of this data be used for the Pulse? What kinds of new medical discoveries would be possible by detailed, real-time monitoring of several health indicators from millions of people? What new basic laws of social interaction on a large scale could be discovered? Could we, like the psychohistorian of Isaac Asimovs science fiction, begin to predict society? Could we predict civil unrest or evolving social morays?

No matter what evolves from these developments, I'm sure we will get used to the Pulse like our own heartbeat. We are going to develop a very different idea of what "connected" really means.

Notes

1. C.J. Hoofnagle, J. King, S. Li, and J. Turow. "How Different Are Young Adults from Older Adults When It Comes to Information Privacy Attitudes and Policies?" April 14, 2010, Social Science Research Network, ssrn.com/abstract=1589864.
2. Wallis Consulting Group. Community Attitudes Towards Privacy 2007, prepared for the Office of the Privacy Commissioner, Australia, 2007, www.privacy. gov.au/materials/types/download/8820/6616.
3. P. Norberg, D. Horne, and D. Horne. "The Privacy Paradox: Personal Information Disclosure Intentions versus Behaviors," *Journal of Consumer Affairs* 41, no. 1 (2007): 100–126.
4. R. Agarwal and C. Anderson. "The Complexity of Consumer Willingness to Disclose Personal Information: Unraveling Health Information Privacy Concerns," Unpublished manuscript, 2008.
5. B. Knispel et. al. "Pulsar Discovery by Global Volunteer Computing," *Science* 329, no. 5997 (September 2010): 1305.
6. E. Korpela et. al. "SETI@home—Massively Distributed Computing for SETI," *Computing in Science & Engineering* 3 (January 2001): 78–83.
7. Michael Culbert. RFID Network Arrangement. Apple Computer, Inc., Cupertino, CA, assignee. Patent 20070054616, March 8, 2007.

About the Author

D OUGLAS W. HUBBARD is the inventor of Applied Information Economics (AIE), a measurement methodology that has earned him critical praise from The Gartner Group, Giga Information Group, and Forrester Research. He is an internationally recognized expert in difficult measurements, valuations of "intangibles" and the application of quantitative methods to decisions under high uncertainty. For more than 20 years, he has applied his expertise in diverse fields such as information technology, military logistics, environmental policy, pharmaceutical product development, the entertainment industry, mergers & acquisitions, military R&D, and engineering project management. He has written articles for *Information Week*, *CIO Enterprise*, and *DBMS Magazine* and is also the author of *The Failure of Risk Management: Why It's Broken and How to Fix It* and *How to Measure Anything: Finding the Value of "Intangibles" in Business, Second Edition*.

Index